# 100 MUST-READ
# AMERICAN
# NOVELS

Nick Rennison and Ed Wood

A & C Black Publishers Ltd

1 3 5 7 9 10 8 6 4 2

First published in 2010

A & C Black Publishers Ltd
36 Soho Square
London W1D 3QY
www.acblack.com.

A CIP catalogue record for this book is available from the British Library

ISBN: 978 1 408 12912 8

Typeset by Margaret Brain, Wisbech, Cambs
Printed and bound in Great Britain by CPI Bookmarque, Croydon, CR0 4TD

# CONTENTS

# ABOUTTHISBOOK

This book is not intended to provide a list of the one hundred 'best' American novels ever published. Given the sheer range of fiction Americans have written in the last two centuries and the unpredictability of individual taste, any such definitive list is an impossibility. Instead we have chosen one hundred books to read which we think will provide some sense of the enormous variety of novels that can be shelved under the heading of 'American Fiction'. We have picked almost exclusively novels but we have also included two collections of short stories by writers (Edgar Allan Poe and Raymond Carver) whose finest work was undoubtedly in the shorter format.

The individual entries in the guide are arranged A to Z by author. They describe the chosen books as concisely as possible (while aiming to avoid too many 'spoilers') and say something briefly about the writer and his or her life and career. Significant film versions of the books (with dates of release) are noted where applicable, followed by '*Read on*' lists comprising books by the same author, books by stylistically similar writers or books on a theme relevant to the main entry. Scattered throughout the text there are also '*Read on a Theme*' menus which list between six and a dozen titles united by a common theme. The symbol ›› before an author name indicates that the author is one of those covered in the A to Z entries.

# INTRODUCTION

When did the writing of American fiction begin? In the colonial period, the novels that existed were English novels, imported from the mother country or printed in cheap (and usually pirated) editions on the printing presses of Boston and Philadelphia. There is scholarly debate about which was the very first American novel but the accolade is usually granted to William Hill Brown's *The Power of Sympathy* which was published in Boston in 1789. Brown's epistolary novel was a pale reflection of the sentimental novel so popular on the other side of the Atlantic and, for the next few decades, the problem with the limited number of American novels that found their way into print was that they struggled to find any indigenous subject for their stories. They were *all* pale reflections of English originals. Susanna Rowson's *Charlotte Temple*, the story of a young woman seduced and brought to America only to be abandoned there, may have been the most popular American bestseller before *Uncle Tom's Cabin* but it followed an English model, was written by a woman who spent long periods of her life in England and was first published in London in 1791, three years before the first American edition appeared in Philadelphia. Charles Brockden Brown, sometimes cited as the first professional American author, was an accomplished novelist and can still be read with interest today but

*Wieland*, his best-known work, published in 1798, is clearly based on English originals, most notably William Godwin's *Caleb Williams*.

The two writers who found a way to escape the 'cultural cringe' of early American fiction were ➤➤ Washington Irving and ➤➤ James Fenimore Cooper. Irving was a great Anglophile but he was also interested in folk tales and the stories that were told in the villages and towns of New England. The results of this interest were Rip Van Winkle and Ichabod Crane. Cooper's 'Leatherstocking Tales', which began to appear in the 1820s, were an offshoot of the historical fiction that proliferated in the wake of Sir Walter Scott. The difference was that Cooper went in search of American history that would provide the same kind of plot potential Scott found in the Middle Ages or the Jacobite Rebellions. He found it in the French and Indian War. One of the consequences was that he (like Irving) became popular in Europe. For the first time, fiction was travelling across the Atlantic from West to East rather than the other way about.

Another writer who found an audience in Europe (although sadly not until after his death) was ➤➤ Edgar Allan Poe. Famously, the French poet Baudelaire was bowled over by the heady atmosphere of Poe's poetry and short fiction and spent much energy in the 1850s translating them into French. For years, Poe's influence abroad was significantly higher than it was in the USA. In the 1830s, when Poe was just beginning his struggle to survive on the income he could gather from publishing his work, another novelist was, like Fenimore Cooper, looking to American history for his subject matter. ➤➤ Nathaniel Hawthorne was to find it in the Puritan inheritance of New England and stories in *Twice-Told Tales* (1837) such as 'The Minister's Black Veil' and 'The May-Pole of Merry Mount' explored the American past with a sophistication and intelligence far beyond anything that Cooper had ever been able to muster. Thirteen years after the publication of *Twice-Told Tales*, Hawthorne produced his masterpiece, *The Scarlet Letter*, which once again found its story in the Puritan past that the author, a direct descendant of one of the judges in the Salem witch trials, found such a painful legacy to contemplate. At the same time Hawthorne's friend >> Herman Melville was working on *Moby-Dick* which was published the year after *The Scarlet Letter*. In the story of Captain Ahab's obsessive search for the whale, Melville found a way of combining the material he had gathered during his days at sea with the brooding allegory and psychological intensity that Hawthorne had manufactured from his Puritan history to produce what was probably the first (and arguably the best) candidate for the much-disputed title of the Great American Novel.

There have been plenty of other claimants to the title down the years. >> Mark Twain's greatest works appeared a quarter of a century and more after the publication of *Moby-Dick*, at a time when Melville, spurned by the literary world, was working as a customs inspector in New York. *The Adventures of Huckleberry Finn* would be on most people's list of Great American Novels, although Twain himself might have mocked the portentousness and pretensions inherent in the use of capital letters. Certainly, by using a first-person narrative in such a distinctively American voice, Twain opened up new ways of telling American stories and he also raised issues – most particularly race – that have been exercising novelists in the USA ever since.

Twain was at pains to emphasise the realism of the accents and voices he gave to his characters in *Huckleberry Finn* and realism, although defined in very different ways, was the new watchword of the American novel. William Dean Howells, often described as the father of

American realism, published *The Rise of Silas Lapham* in 1885. This story of the fluctuating fortunes, both financial and moral, of a self-made millionaire in upper-class Boston, was Howells' antidote to the sentimentality with which he believed much of American fiction was afflicted. As the powerful editor of *The Atlantic Monthly*, he was in a strong position to impose his taste on the literary world. Meanwhile, in a European exile that he relished, ›› Henry James was employing his own particular version of psychological realism in the minute study of the culture clashes that occurred when the New World met the Old.

One of the younger writers that Henry James most admired was ›› Stephen Crane whose short and meteoric career in the 1890s most famously produced the finest novel of the Civil War (*The Red Badge of Courage*) but also initiated a new era of naturalism in American fiction. Apart from *The Red Badge of Courage*, Crane's other major achievement was *Maggie: A Girl of the Streets*, which focused on the lives of boozers and prostitutes in New York's Bowery district. This was the European naturalism of writers like Emile Zola given a uniquely American twist. Crane was followed by Frank Norris, another novelist who died young, with works like *McTeague* and *The Octopus*, and by ›› Theodore Dreiser with *Sister Carrie*. In 1906, the avowedly socialist writer Upton Sinclair, who nursed the ambition to write 'the *Uncle Tom's Cabin* of the labor movement', published *The Jungle*, a savage indictment of the Chicago meat-packing business. The vast expansion of industrial America and the urban squalor it produced demanded some response in fiction and it received it in the work of these self-consciously naturalistic writers.

However, a new way of interpreting the world was in the air. Only three years after the publication of *The Jungle*, Gertrude Stein wrote

*Three Lives*, arguably the first work of American modernist fiction. Realism was no longer enough. The First World War fragmented writers' visions of art and culture and the meaning of the world even further. America may have entered the war in Europe only for its last eighteen months but an astonishingly high proportion of the writers who shaped modernism took some part in it. Most of them ended up, like Gertrude Stein, living in exile in Paris in the 1920s. Eccentrics like Djuna Barnes, author of *Nightwood*, one of the strangest and most entrancing works of the period, as well as those like ›› Ernest Hemingway and ›› F. Scott Fitzgerald who now take up many more pages in the literary histories of that era, briefly found a spiritual home in France. Others like ›› William Faulkner and ›› John Dos Passos, who had been in Europe during the war, returned home to the USA to create their own versions of modernism. Faulkner's fiction, with its fusion of modernist techniques and the already long tradition of Southern literature, proved particularly remarkable.

The 1920s also saw another, hugely significant development – the creation of a new African-American literature. There had long been individual works by black writers (Charles Chesnutt's *The Marrow of Tradition*, for example, was a 1900 novel which explored the complicated realities of a so-called race riot) but there had been nothing to compare with the coming together of writers, artists and musicians in New York which became known as the Harlem Renaissance. This flowering of African-American intellectual life included novelists such as ›› Zora Neale Hurston (*Their Eyes Were Watching God*), Jean Toomer (*Cane*) and Claude McKay (*Home to Harlem*).

The same decade also witnessed the beginnings of distinctively American genre fiction. Crime fiction sprang in part from the work of

**»** Edgar Allan Poe nearly a century earlier but it had become naturalised in Europe where Sherlock Holmes and the detectives who followed in his wake had cornered the market. Now the pulp magazines of the 1920s and 1930s became the home for a new style of 'hardboiled' fiction, pioneered by the likes of **»** Dashiell Hammett, that could only be American in origin. Poe had also been one of the earliest exponents of what would now be called science fiction but this genre too had emigrated to France (the works of Jules Verne) and to England (the scientific romances of H.G. Wells). Now it too returned as Hugo Gernsback founded the first magazine (*Amazing Stories*) devoted to it in 1926 and even created the term 'science fiction' to describe what he was publishing.

As the 1920s turned into the 1930s, modernism ran out of steam. The Wall Street Crash of 1929 drove America into the Great Depression and a new form of socially conscious realism seemed necessary to depict the consequences. The ironies and the experimentation of the Jazz Age and novels like **The Great Gatsby** now looked flippant and irresponsible in the face of the suffering that economic disaster inflicted on so many people. Writers like **»** John Steinbeck (*Cannery Row*, *Of Mice and Men*, *The Grapes of Wrath*) and James T. Farrell (the Studs Lonigan trilogy about a working-class protagonist in Chicago's South Side) seemed more in tune with the spirit of the age.

The Depression years were, of course, followed by the Second World War. Unlike in Britain, where the war seemed to stimulate literary culture in unprecedented ways, the years between 1941 and 1945 were years of stasis in American fiction. However, no sooner was the war over and won, than the race to write the Great American War Novel began. **»** Gore Vidal was an early entrant with his debut novel, **Williwaw**, published in 1946. ›› Norman Mailer weighed in (the verb is perhaps significant in view of the size of the book) with *The Naked and the Dead* in 1948. Other war novels followed in the 1950s, such as James Jones's *From Here to Eternity* and Herman Wouk's *The Caine Mutiny*, which were written by participants struggling to make sense of what they had witnessed, but the genre culminated in the black comedy of ›› Joseph Heller's *Catch-22* (1961) which refused to admit that there was any sense there to find.

The post-war period saw two decades of unprecedented prosperity in America, and with it a 'white flight' into the suburbs in the 1950s. Perfect little homes with neat yards seemed to embody the achievement of the American Dream, but the mundanity and uniformity of life in these Protestant, middle-class environments began to concern writers like ›› John Updike, ›› John Cheever and ›› Richard Yates, who found them divorced from the actualities of modern industrial and multi-ethnic life and an unhappily homogenising influence upon individual identity. Updike's Rabbit Angstrom in *Rabbit, Run* (1960), Yates' Frank Wheeler in *Revolutionary Road* (1955) and Cheever's Coverly Wapshot in *The Wapshot Chronicle* (1957) are men for whom the suburbs have meant turmoil and disappointment, rather than comfort. It's a theme returned to time and again by writers from slumbering small-towns in the Midwest and North East like ›› John Irving, ›› Richard Ford and ›› Jonathan Franzen, who created character-driven monuments to America's past exemplifying its slowly changing neighbourhoods, individuals and attitudes.

Some writers went further, presenting small-town thinking as downright sinister. ›› Shirley Jackson drew on her own ostracism in her Vermont hometown and fused it with Gothic horror for her disturbing stories of the 1940s–60s. Later, in ›› Jeffrey Eugenides' *The Virgin Suicides* (1993) and ›› Stephen King's *Carrie* (1974), suburban America's conscience appears to have been almost entirely swallowed up by rabid religiosity and an uncurious timidity that shuns difference – King, of course, mined a rich seam of horror from his fascination with small-town America to build one of the bestselling bodies of work of the century.

In the mid-1950s and 1960s, a sense of outrage ballooned forth from the big cities in outright rejection of the old-fashioned American values so driven by the interests and ambitions of the older generation. While literature had, for the most part, been a middle-class pursuit for most of the century, these two decades saw working-class young men speaking out, dropping out, or fighting back. The counterculture movement threw up poets, junkies, bums and barflies and made stars of them. Beat friends ›› Jack Kerouac, Allen Ginsberg and ›› William S. Burroughs transformed views of what literature could be: not for them elitist Queen's English – their writings were crude, rammed with dialect and slang, and buzzed with the excitement of artificial highs and the optimism of youth. ›› Kerouac's *On The Road* (1957) and ›› J.D. Salinger's *The Catcher in the Rye* (1951) espoused the power of youth to change the new America – but, crucially, neither ignored how that change would effect those young people or how lost they would feel pursuing it. Their new visions jettisoned sleepy acceptance for a tirade of angst and questioning – a mode also picked up in the cinema of the mid-1950s with *The Wild One* and *Rebel Without A Cause* – and helped to change not only the course of literature, but also the way in which America saw itself. For them though, youth was rebellion; it was an escape from the generation that had taken America into war.

That sense of rebellion continued in two major takes on the Second

World War, astonishingly original pieces of work that employed bleak satirical humour and non-linear storytelling to convey the absurdity of death on a mass scale. >> Joseph Heller's *Catch-22* and *Slaughterhouse-Five* by >> Kurt Vonnegut (1969) – both by men who had experienced war's insanity first-hand – were bitter attacks on the irrationality of command decisions. The literary experimentation of these books reflected – as did >> Burroughs' work – the leaping of literature into the wild blue yonder of postmodernism. A stream of thought prefigured by post-structuralist French thinkers such as Michel Foucault and matured by the likes of Jacques Derrida, it focused on the creation of the means of understanding (or 'signs') and how that process defines that understanding – for example, how the surface level of language is the limit of our knowledge of the world. Amalgamating with the new frontiers opened up by groundbreaking modernist writers from >> Melville and Joyce to >> Faulkner, Nabokov and innovative Argentine author Jorge Luis Borges, this thinking saw postmodern American writers playing with the very idea of fiction as a means of storytelling, breaking down the barriers between the author, their subject and the reader, and transforming existing genres into playful new forms freed from a central narrative structure. Spearheading postmodern literature's first flowering was >> Thomas Pynchon. Like >> Heller and >> Vonnegut, he used postmodernism's chaotic, transgressive nature to speak about the unspeakable. *Gravity's Rainbow* (1973) is a long, digressive, sexually-demented wartime story that reads like nothing written before or since, yet Pynchon's influence can be seen in any number of writers right up to today.

But if it sounds as if the whole literary world was involved in a high-flown collective postmodern endeavour, the truth is that realism as a style still dominated as a powerful means of expression for those who were otherwise ignored by society. The blue-collar guys who kept the country running were still there and, just as ›› Hemingway had done decades earlier, they employed direct and powerful prose to convey the realities of working-class lives. The stories of ›› Charles Bukowski and ›› Raymond Carver are bound up in the miserable childhoods that had led them down bad roads slick with booze and bust-ups. Bukowski's novels were autobiographical tales of sexual violence and personal degradation in the working-man's world; Carver's writing found a delicate poetry and minimalist tenor that transformed the art of short story for good. Both, however, perceived alcohol both as escape and cruel mistress – just as ›› Faulkner had – and the failings of fathers as having ripped at the seams of society.

Booze also soaked the pages of the big cities' new lyricists of murder as a new gang of hardboiled crime writers emerged that had lived lives as grim and squalid as those they portrayed. Elmore Leonard, Jim Thompson and ›› James Ellroy all had problems with alcohol (among other things) and the murders in their stories seem to spring from a bleak misanthropy born of grimy city life. In their cities, whether it's Leonard's Detroit or Ellroy's LA, modern America itself is a flawed concept built on the bodies of those ignored by the corrupt and powerful.

The mass of the ignored had already begun to speak through literature before the war, but fiction by women, ethnic minorities and the gay community pressed home the civil rights campaigning that swept the country in the 1960s. ›› Sylvia Plath's *The Bell Jar* (1963) presented a New York in which women could now claim independence and hold glamorous, exciting jobs, but where depression was treated with electro-shock therapy and women were heaped with behavioural expectations. ➤➤ Judy Blume's literature for young teen girls helped to transform these expectations for good, introducing a generation of girls to the realities of womanhood, starting with *Are You There God? It's Me, Margaret* (1970) and continuing with *Forever* (1975). Her candid approach jolted a shocked Christian Right into proclaiming her books unsuitable for children, reflecting an ongoing battle for taboo-busting novels trying to advance empathy and common understanding.

A similar story is true of writing about the black experience. While ➤➤ Harper Lee's charming, stirring story about racial injustice in 1930s Alabama, *To Kill a Mockingbird* (1960), became one of the most popular books in the English language, other books dealing with harsh realities for African-Americans achieved the same level of controversy as ➤➤ Richard Wright's *Native Son* had done in 1940. But now, post-civil rights, post-Martin Luther King, post-feminism, women were at last at the forefront of racial and gender dialogue in literature. Like *To Kill a Mockingbird*, ➤➤ Alice Walker's *The Color Purple* (1982) and ➤➤ Toni Morrison's *Beloved* (1988) exposed continuing racial tensions in the modern South by exploring the legacy of slavery, in their cases specifically by portraying the horrors inflicted upon disenfranchised African-American women in rural communities. Both are critically-acclaimed bestsellers, yet are also among the most challenged or banned books in the USA. Absolutely truthful in their brutality and emotional engagement with their female protagonists, these books have been vital milestones in the formation of modern African-American identity and in confronting the nation with the bloody building blocks of its rise.

As women and African-Americans found their voice in literature, so too did LGBT writers. The Stonewall riots in New York (1969) and the rise of Harvey Milk in San Francisco saw the gay community grabbing a political platform. Like Milk, author ➤➤ Armistead Maupin was a member of San Francisco's flourishing gay community of the time; like Milk, he was responsible for public acknowledgement of the gay lifestyle. Gay characters had, of course, appeared previously in work by gay authors, such as ➤➤ Patricia Highsmith's self-deceiving amoral killer in *The Talented Mr Ripley*, but Maupin's *Tales of the City* (1978) showed that, finally, mainstream readers were ready to read about sympathetic and happily sexually-active gay characters, overturning the kinds of homophobic attitudes seen in ➤➤ Annie Proulx's 1960s and '70s-set short story 'Brokeback Mountain' – though right-wing reactions to the 2005 film adaptation of the story suggest that Milk's battle is nowhere near won.

In the post-war period, Jewish writers too made their mark, just as the true horror of the Holocaust was coming to light (it's perhaps not coincidental that ➤➤ Henry Roth's *Call it Sleep* (1934), about Austrian-Jewish immigrants in New York, only found its audience after the war). American novelists have continually found inventive and shocking new ways of portraying the genocide: ➤➤ Jerzy Kosinki's *The Painted Bird* (1965) fictionalised his own traumatised journey through a devastated Europe as a child of the war; ➤➤ Art Spiegelman's Pulitzer Prize-winning graphic novel *MAUS* (1992) used animal allegory; ➤➤ Jonathan Safran Foer's *Everything Is Illuminated* (2002) wrapped facts within fictions in a postmodern search for identity decades after the genocide.

As individualism became the defining nature of American society, that question of identity drove the Jewish-American writers who created new candidates for the title of the Great American Novel – if *The Great Gatsby* was about the creation of an individual's invented identity, then novels by Jewish-Americans came to dominate fictional debates about the formation of American identity in its immigrant totality. The touchstone is ➤➤ Saul Bellow's landmark novel *The Adventures of Augie March* (1953), the story of a wandering soul searching for the American Dream and never finding it. Bellow's unparalleled award-winning success threw long shadows across the following decades, most of all inspiring ➤➤ Philip Roth, his pupil in Chicago and one of the most significant authors of the second half of the twentieth century. The controversy-courting masturbatory comedy *Portnoy's Complaint* (1969) announced the arrival of an author who would command column inches, literary prizes and the bestseller charts for the best part of four decades; for the first two of those, his novels displayed a fleet-footed self-reflexivity inspired by postmodern writing, and many featured his alter-ego Nathan Zuckerman – they also left many wondering whether Roth was an outright misogynist, a genius or simply a faker. A stylistic about-turn in the 1990s saw a maturity and obsession with mortality enter his work, most significantly in *American Pastoral* (1997). Roth had always questioned the American Dream, but here it was explicit, placing the blame for social disorder at the feet of the 1960s, the decade that had produced all of those pioneering new voices. Ironically, as those given voices by the civil rights movements of that decade had done, assimilation was the cultural conclusion: thanks to ➤➤ Bellow and Roth – as well as other leading Jewish writers like ➤➤ Michael Chabon – the Jew was no longer a metaphor for wandering or tragedy: he (and in these works it is 'he') was American.

In the epic sweep of chronology and theme, the Great American Novel as we think of it was born of these immigrant tales, stories that tried to make sense of the nation's state, history and future, at a time when the political and cultural ethics of America were brought into question by the Vietnam War and the Cold War. The tragic-comic suburban subversions of the American Dream of the 1950s hardened in the following decades into tougher novels that held a gun to the heart of the nation's self-image. ➤➤ Cormac McCarthy drew on the Southern Gothic of ➤➤ Faulkner to dispel mythologies of America's frontier expansion in his sanguinary Westerns, of which *Blood Meridian* (1985) is a particularly distressing example – like ➤➤ Toni Morrison, his poetic prose was aimed fully at exposing the contradiction between the white man's self-interested creation of the American Dream with the means by which he achieved it. ➤➤ Don DeLillo, meanwhile, took his cues from ➤➤ Pynchon for sprawling novels like *White Noise* (1985) and *Underworld* (1997) that looked hard into the soul of the country. Using real events overlaid with fictions DeLillo presented, like ➤➤ Roth, America as a family in crisis, beset on all sides by religious, consumerist and psycho-sexual obsessions.

This sense of crisis had been building for decades, providing impetus for science-fiction writers who wondered what might have been as a way of examining what was. ➤➤ Ray Bradbury's *Fahrenheit 451* (1953) pictured a US in which books were banned and television had become the only acceptable artistic outlet. ➤➤ Philip K. Dick's alternative history *The Man in the High Castle* (1962) imagined an America after the Axis powers had won the war, transforming race relations but, in some ways, only exacerbating a mode of thought present in the Deep South; Dick's book found a parallel tale in ➤➤ Philip Roth's picture of an isolationist, anti-Semitic country in *The Plot Against America* (2004). ➤➤ Ursula K. Le Guin took to other worlds with *The Left Hand of Darkness* (1969), but her invention of a genderless society living without war being encroached upon by a benign human empire spoke loudly about gender and politics in a country then divided over intervention in a foreign land. And ›› William Gibson's genre-creating cyberpunk novel *Neuromancer* (1984) extended the pell-mell digital progress and body fetishisation of the 1980s into a nightmarish near future.

In the 1980s, Reagan's America fostered unique satirical novels aimed at pricking the consciences of the big-city power-dressers creaming the profits of a Wall Street boom while the streets became more dangerous. The era's chief satirist was ›› Tom Wolfe, a writer who'd gained attention as a pioneer of New Journalism, the reporting style that made the name of such cultural icons as Joan Didion and Hunter S. Thompson. Wolfe's first novel came twenty years after he became famous, but *The Bonfire of the Vanities* (1987) quickly established themes that were to recur in 1980s and early 1990s fiction from ›› Bret Easton Ellis to ›› Jay McInerney and ›› Chuck Palahniuk: greed, drugs, masculinity in crisis and the pitiless treatment of the little guy.

In employing the tricks and trappings of postmodernism, these authors were part of a golden age for a style that has continued to the present day. ›› Paul Auster, in particular, began a significant career with the head-spinning metafictional detective novel *The New York Trilogy* (1987), whose influence is clearly visible in ›› Jonathan Lethem's peculiar crime-genre-bender *Motherless Brooklyn* (1999), while the existentialist angst of Auster's opaque characters can be seen in Joshua Ferris' *The Unnamed* (2010). Postmodernism has, in the past decade, shown itself to be an infinitely flexible style through which to examine numerous issues affecting modern America: addiction and grief (James Frey's fictive non-fiction *A Million Little Pieces*, 2003); the dynamic of the office (Joshua Ferris' *Then We Came to the End*, 2007) the 9/11 attacks (>> Dave Eggers' *Extremely Loud and Incredibly Close*, 2005). Yet critics seem to be tiring of the inherent authorial self-interest of postmodernism, and some recent literary bestsellers, such as >> Jonathan Franzen's *The Corrections* (2001) and >> Donna Tartt's *The Secret History* (1992) would suggest the rude health of old-fashioned storytelling. More pressing is the effect that the digital revolution will have on the novel form: perhaps portable small-screen reading could revolutionise the fortunes of the short story; maybe the innovation of visual writing – where typographic design elements are part of the storytelling, a method pioneered by cult author Mark Z. Danielewski in *House of Leaves* (2000) and also seen in Eggers' book – will further develop in a touch-screen environment.

'I cannot live without books', Thomas Jefferson wrote. While the rise of the e-book might see the physical artefact assuming a new role or metamorphosing, the power of American literature to define, question and guide the country he led two centuries ago will never fade.

# A–ZOF ENTRIES

## JAMES AGEE (1909–55)

### A DEATH IN THE FAMILY (1957)

In his lifetime, James Agee was best known as a film critic and writer of screenplays (he produced scripts for two of the most admired American films of the 1950s, *The African Queen* and *The Night of the Hunter*) but his posthumous reputation is based largely on his autobiographical novel, *A Death in the Family*. Agee began work on it in the late 1940s and it was close to completion when he died of a heart attack in 1955. The book is set in 1915 and examines, in closely observed detail, the immediate consequences for his family of the death of a man named Jay Follett in a car accident. At the centre of the book is the man's young son Rufus (a character clearly based on Agee himself whose own father was killed in very similar circumstances when the writer was a boy) and it is through Rufus's eyes that readers first see the impact of sudden death. Yet Agee also shifts his focus as his narrative continues. Like a movie camera panning across a group of people and then zooming in on just one, he pays attention to other members of the family. We see the differing reactions to Jay's death of his wife, Mary, struggling to accommodate it in her religious view of life, and of her father, grimly confident that it confirms him in his atheism. In a brilliant and extended scene, we witness the stumbling efforts of Andrew, Mary's brother, to break the news of the death. We are even allowed to share the puzzlement of Rufus's younger sister as the toddler half-grasps the significance of what has happened. 'The work of a writer whose power with English words can make you gasp', as one critic described it at the time of publication, *A Death in the Family* is a lyrical and moving exploration of death and grief.

◀ **Film version:** *All the Way Home* (1963)

📖 **Read on**
*Let Us Now Praise Famous Men* (Agee produced this extraordinary record of the lives of poor sharecroppers in Alabama in collaboration with the photographer Walker Evans)
➤➤ William Maxwell, *They Came Like Swallows*

# LOUISA MAY ALCOTT (1832–88)

## LITTLE WOMEN (1868/9)
The daughter of Bronson Alcott, a renowned American educationalist, Louisa May Alcott published more than two hundred books in her lifetime but is mostly remembered for just one – *Little Women*. Following the fortunes of Meg, Jo, Beth and Amy March, the daughters

of an army chaplain absent in the American Civil War, the novel begins as they all gather in the family living room to talk and goes on to record both the everyday pleasures and the trials and tribulations of their lives. Tomboyish Jo, a would-be writer based on Alcott herself, has the excitement of getting a story published. The wealthy Mr Laurence and his grandson Laurie become neighbours and close friends of the family. Amy and Jo quarrel and Amy burns one of her sister's manuscripts. Laurie's young tutor falls in love with Meg. At one point, a telegram arrives with the bad news that Mr March is hospitalised in Washington DC and Mrs March, partly financed by money from the sale of Jo's hair, is obliged to travel there to look after him. As the girls progress from teenage years to young womanhood, they are obliged to face the prospects of love and work and premature death. The saintly Beth contracts scarlet fever while visiting sick neighbours and has to battle with terminal illness. Laurie proposes to Jo but she turns him down. The narrative wends its way towards a concluding scene in which the surviving girls, older and wiser, meet together once more to give thanks for what life and sisterhood has given them. Alcott wrote two sequels to *Little Women* (*Little Men* and *Jo's Boys*) and its story has been adapted and re-told as everything from films (twelve of them at the last count) to an opera, from a Classics Illustrated comic to Japanese anime. It has become one of the archetypal narratives of American fiction.

**◄Film versions:** *Little Women* (1933, directed by George Cukor and starring Katharine Hepburn as Jo); *Little Women* (1949, starring Elizabeth Taylor as Amy and June Allyson as Jo); *Little Women* (1994, starring Winona Ryder as Jo)

**≋Read on**

*Little Men*; *Jo's Boys*

Geraldine Brooks, *March* (a modern Pulitzer Prize-winning novel which takes the father of Alcott's March family as its central character); Susan Coolidge, *What Katy Did*, Laura Ingalls Wilder, *The Little House on the Prairie*

# PAUL AUSTER (b. 1947)

## THE NEW YORK TRILOGY (1987)

Paul Auster is a pioneer of postmodern metafiction and master storyteller who has written screenplays, non-fiction and poetry as well as novels – carefully crafted works that pose questions about the self, reality and meaning. His debut novel, *The New York Trilogy* – published when Auster was already forty – provided a near-flawless calling card. The book comprises three stories written during the early to mid-1980s: *City of Glass*, in which a crime writer poses as a detective after receiving a mistaken late-night phone call to the 'Auster Detective Agency'; *Ghosts*, in which a detective named Blue spies on Black for a client named White, in the process losing his own identity; and *The Locked Room*, about a writer who takes the credit for an unpublished book written by his vanished friend Fanshawe. Like an Ouroboros, Auster's stories eat themselves to form a never-ending loop of fiction within fiction within fiction. As in all his writing, randomness plays a hand in the characters' lives, while much goes unsaid: the effect is disconcerting, thrumming with underlying menace, as in the plays of Harold Pinter or a dark fairytale. Indeed, Auster's works have elements of modern fairytale: the man who can fly in *Mr Vertigo*; the mysterious notebook seller in *Oracle Night*; the lost film of a screen actor in *The Book of Illusions*. Part of the joy, however, is they're also surprisingly warm and redemptive – fiction is, for Auster, both prison-guard and redeemer. In *The New York Trilogy* you can sense Auster trying everything out at once in a one-off, unrepeatable deconstruction of crime fiction; though the 'crimes', such as they are, happen off-stage, here is the man-on-a-wire tautness of ›› Raymond Chandler and ›› Dashiell Hammett, played out in metaphysical explorations of how surveillance works both as a real and fictional-literary concept. The sensation is not of a novelist demolishing the Brechtian fourth wall, but of fiction seeping into the cracks and furrows of real life. Auster makes us all the subjects of our own novels.

## Read on
*The Book of Illusions*; *Moon Palace*; *The Music of Chance*
Nicholson Baker, *The Mezzanine*; ›› Don DeLillo, *White Noise*

# JAMES BALDWIN (1924–87)

## GO TELL IT ON THE MOUNTAIN (1953)

Once described as 'one of the few genuinely indispensable American writers', James Baldwin was exploring issues of race and sexuality in society long before they came to the attention of the wider culture. Both black and gay, he confronted prejudice and overturned expectations in his work which eventually consisted of half a dozen novels, plays, poetry, short stories and (perhaps most importantly) collections of fiery and uncompromising essays such as *Notes of a Native Son* and *The Fire Next Time*. Long an exile in Europe, Baldwin was a powerful voice crying in the wilderness throughout the 1950s and the 1960s. His best-known fiction belongs to the earlier decade. *Giovanni's Room*, published in 1956, is about an American in Paris, having to choose between his mistress and his (male) lover. *Go Tell It on the Mountain*, his debut novel, is about a poor Harlem family torn apart by the pressures of born-again Christianity. 'Everyone had always said that John would be a preacher when he grew up, just like his father,' the book begins and it follows the story of the crisis John Grimes faces as he reaches his fourteenth birthday. Partly this is a religious crisis but John's problems lie more with his relationship with the man he believes to be his father, a harsh and unbending preacher named Gabriel. John longs for his father's love but also hates him and what he represents. As the novel unfolds, the reader learns of Gabriel's history in flashback and knows that the preacher is a deeply flawed man but John does not and he must endure a long dark night of the soul alone. Like many a first novel, *Go Tell It on the Mountain* draws heavily on the author's own experiences of growing up but there is no disputing the power of what Baldwin himself later called, 'the book I had to write if I was ever going to write anything else'.

🐟**Read on**
*Another Country*; *Giovanni's Room*; *The Fire Next Time* (essays on race in America)
John Edgar Wideman, *Hiding Place*; ›› Richard Wright, *Native Son*

# SAUL BELLOW (1915–2005)

## THE ADVENTURES OF AUGIE MARCH (1953)

Saul Bellow was one of America's most garlanded authors, winning the Nobel Prize in 1976, the Pulitzer Prize in 1975 for *Humboldt's Gift*, and the National Book Award a record three times, including once for *The Adventures of Augie March*. He has inspired writers from Martin Amis to Philip Roth. Yet this literary colossus came from the kind of humble origins that exemplify the American experience. Born to poor Russian-Jewish parents in Canada in 1915, he moved with his family to Chicago in 1924, the setting for many of his novels. Married five times, Bellow was an intellectual polyglot who aimed in his fiction at answering the ultimate question of, as he said in his Nobel acceptance lecture, 'what we human beings are ... and what this life is for'. Bellow's picaresque third novel *Augie March* exemplifies that existential search. When we meet young Augie, his immigrant household – lacking a father – is already crumbling: later, returning after a spell away from Chicago in which the Depression looms large, it will collapse. Throughout the novel Augie seeks to create something better than the path fate – or others – lays out for him, but rarely succeeds: he wants to be loved, is easily led and has a 'weak sense of consequence'. 'People would feel the world owed me distinctness,' Augie says, yet in his moth-like flitting he fails to find that calling. Like a painting by Jackson Pollock, *Augie March* is exuberant, scattershot and full of texture. Bellow's prose is dense with (sometimes jaw-dropping) detail, especially in its hyper-formed human zoo of characters. But he's also able to pare back to moments of terrible poignancy, such as during the committing of Augie's mentally disabled younger brother Georgie. Meanwhile, verbal colloquialisms and leaps of descriptive fancy carry the book far beyond the formalism of his earlier work. Augie is human through and through and so, like real life, the book offers no easy resolution – the American Dream is not so easily fulfilled. And yet, as the celebrated opening says, he remains 'an American, Chicago born ... and go at things as I have taught myself, free-style, and will make the record in my own way ...'

## ⮧Read on
*Henderson the Rain King*; *Herzog*; *Humboldt's Gift*
» Bernard Malamud, *Dubin's Lives*; » Philip Roth, *Sabbath's Theater*;
» Henry Roth, *Call It Sleep*

# THOMAS BERGER (b. 1924)

## LITTLE BIG MAN (1964)

Think of Western fiction and the image that probably comes to mind is that of the dime novel and its descendants – cheap, luridly jacketed paperbacks in which Billy the Kid blasts his shotguns at his enemies or Buffalo Bill battles against the Indians. In fact, there is also a long tradition in American literature of more sophisticated novels about the West. One of the cleverest and most knowing of all such books is Thomas Berger's *Little Big Man* in which the author combined historical accuracy with riotous burlesque to create a tall tale told by his central character, 111-year-old Jack Crabb, looking back on his long life. Born white but adopted into an Indian family, Crabb (or Little Big Man as he is to the Cheyenne) is able to bear witness for the peoples on both sides of the frontier. As Berger's novel unfolds, his hero recounts his meetings with all the legendary figures of the American West. He tangles with Wyatt Earp and rides with Wild Bill Hickok. During his time with the Cheyenne he marries and becomes a father but both his wife and his child are killed in a cavalry raid led by the dementedly charismatic George Armstrong Custer. Little Big Man vows to kill Custer in revenge but the twists and turns of fate take him once again across the boundary between the world of the white man and the world of the Indian, and he finds himself working as a scout for the Seventh Cavalry. As a result, the centenarian can make his most outrageous claim of all – that he is the sole white survivor of the Battle of the Little Big Horn and Custer's Last Stand. Thomas Berger is one of the most versatile American novelists of his generation and his picaresque saga of the Old

West, as it might have been but probably wasn't, is the most entertaining of all his works.

◀**Film version:** *Little Big Man* (1970, starring Dustin Hoffman as Jack Crabb)

📖**Read on**
*Arthur Rex*; *Reinhart in Love*; *The Return of Little Big Man*
Allan Gurganus, *Oldest Living Confederate Widow Tells All*

## JUDY BLUME (b. 1938)

### ARE YOU THERE GOD? IT'S ME, MARGARET (1970)
Judy Blume's seminal book *Are You There God? It's Me, Margaret* is the only teen book in this volume, but for good reason: for a generation of girls Judy Blume provided their first experience of reading where they were not treated as a child. Such is the reverence for Blume that, in 2004, she was awarded the National Book Foundation Medal for Distinguished Contribution to American Letters, an award previously won by ›› John Updike, ›› Saul Bellow and ›› Toni Morrison. Blume was born in 1938 and grew up with her Jewish parents in Elizabeth, New Jersey. She began writing when she had young children; 1970 kicked off a decade of bestsellers with the genuinely groundbreaking *Are You*

*There God?*, which saw Blume become the first writer to talk to girls frankly about boys, sex and puberty. Like much landmark American fiction, the book is about the search for identity among conflicting interests: religious, age and gender based. Its heroine is the nearly 12-year-old only child Margaret, whose Jewish mother and Christian father move them from New York to suburban New Jersey, much to her worry. In fact, she makes new friends like feminine Nancy Wheeler, and with them discovers teenagedom with all of its implicit body-consciousness: 'We must – we must – we must increase our bust!' they chant. But ultimately her most important relationship is with God, though whether he's Jewish or Christian she's unsure. Blume's funny, frothy book – she is particularly witty on the irrationality of adults – is unquestionably a very American phenomenon, so it must be especially hurtful that it's in her home country that her book has been one of the most censored in the Christian Right's effort to smother sex education (ironically Margaret is devotedly religious). Taboo-busting, scrupulously honest and immensely empowering for the girls who devoured it under the duvet with a torch, *Are You There God?* let the cat out of the bag: the effect of Blume's book was like Elvis's pelvis wiggle for an earlier generation. Many of the novels covered in this book write about coming of age: Blume's was a formative part of it.

## 📖Read on

*Forever*
Stephen Chbosky, *The Perks of Being a Wallflower*; Paula Danziger, *The Cat Ate My Gymsuit*; Nicola Keegan, *Swimming*

# T.C. BOYLE (b. 1948)

## WORLD'S END (1987)

Tom Coraghessan Boyle's life skidded off the rails from an early age, a product of his suburban 1960s upbringing in upstate New York at the hands of alcoholic parents. His adult life began with hard drugs and drink, but also a love for music and countercultural literature. The latter turned his life around, via creative writing, academia and a friendship with >> Raymond Carver. His style, however, is far from the scything minimalism of Carver: rambunctious and darkly funny, Boyle stands among the greats, but is also unashamedly entertaining. Perhaps his most acclaimed long work (his short stories are also critical favourites), *World's End* won the PEN/Faulkner award in 1988. Taking as its location Northern Westchester County, the region Boyle grew up in, *World's End* is a multigenerational, chronologically sprawling novel that draws direct links between the displacement of Native Americans by the Dutch in the late seventeeth century, the Peterskill (a fictional version of his hometown Peekskill) McCarthyite riots of 1949, and the political and social upheavals of 1968. Into this Boyle injects genuine human yearning, as accident-prone 22-year-old Walter Van Brunt (he loses a foot in the book's opening) searches for his absent father Truman. Haunted by ghosts, he uncovers their family's grim past in both the seventeenth and the twentieth century, in the process allowing his own life to hit the skids. Despite having a narrative spanning 300 years, *World's End* manages to be both fleet-footed and coherent. Lushly sensory and exuberant in its love of language, the book reads like a grim fairytale in which historical events, paternal love and family shame are spun into one compelling tapestry that questions the role of heredity in fate and free will. On a micro-level, it's the story of one man and his father; on the larger scale, it exposes humanity's never-changing self-centredness so that, as in Gábriel García Marquez's *One Hundred Years of Solitude* or David Mitchell's *Cloud Atlas*, events far apart seem to echo down the generations and forward, into modern America and the present.

## ≋Read on

*Drop City*; *The Road to Wellville*; *The Women*
John Barth, *The Sot-Weed Factor*; ›› Thomas Pynchon, *Mason & Dixon*

# RAY BRADBURY (b. 1920)

## FAHRENHEIT 451 (1953)

Ray Bradbury's career was founded on a happy family-led childhood in Waukegan, Illinois, which he often fictionalised as the sleepy Green Town. Later, as a teen in LA, he published a fanzine and submitted stories to science-fiction magazines; 1950's *The Martian Chronicles* confirmed his talent, exhibiting a very American anxiety over the way that social divides, Cold War paranoia and political distrust had displaced the world of his peaceful childhood. *Fahrenheit 451* came three years later, an Orwellian glimpse at a future in which the written word has been banned. Guy Montag is a 'fireman', but rather than putting out fires his job is to burn books, assisted by a crew of blue-collar guys led by the threatening Beatty and a Mechanical Hound that kills by lethal injection. Montag's life is fragile: his wife Mildred swallows a bottle of sleeping pills, saved only by a standard mobile blood transfusion; the Hound is behaving oddly aggressively to him; and he has something hidden in his home that's making him edgy. Then Montag meets his kooky free-spirited 16-year-old neighbour Clarisse and his eyes are opened. Bradbury's novel turns America on its head: firemen start fires; man's best friend is a robotic killer; advanced medical technology robs medics of knowledge. More than a simple anti-censorship tract, Bradbury's book warns against the depersonalisation of modern life brought about by mutual fear, social controls and the technological and pharmaceutical advancements that destroy humans' natural states, from sleep to conversation. Written at the height of McCarthyism, *Fahrenheit 451* is short, poetic slap in the face to a nation sliding into thought-policing. In keeping with Bradbury's interests, the book is profoundly cinematic, sometimes too much so: there is a tendency for his hyper-descriptiveness to slip into purple prose. Nevertheless, *Fahrenheit 451* is America's *Nineteen Eighty-Four*, its brevity increasingly a virtue when, as its author predicted, communication has become ever more fractured in the face of instant entertainment and homogenised culture, and when the concern of offending special interest groups has indeed impacted on freedom of speech. At the end, however, it is also hopeful, as literature survives beyond the existence of its society.

📼**Film version:** *Fahrenheit 451* (1966, directed by François Truffaut)

📖**Read on**
*Dandelion Wine*; *The Martian Chronicles*; *Something Wicked This Way Comes*
Isaac Asimov, *I, Robot*; ›› Philip K. Dick, *Do Androids Dream of Electric Sheep?*; Walter M. Miller, *A Canticle for Leibovitz*


# CHARLES BUKOWSKI (1920–94)

## HAM ON RYE (1982)
German-born Bukowski was taken to the USA at the age of two in 1923, living first in Baltimore, then LA. His ex-serviceman father was a drinker and a bully and, like him, Henry Charles fell in and out of unskilled jobs and became wed to the bottle, even living rough at times. But the son also had a gift – he could write. Bukowki produced more than forty published works, the best known of which – *Post Office*, *Factotum* and *Ham on Rye* – feature his alter ego, Henry (Hank) Chinaski. The autobiographical *Ham on Rye*, published when Bukowki was 62, follows Henry from timid small boy to mouthy young man, his attitude born of frequent beatings from his thuggish milkman father and the brutality of other kids. Henry becomes tough simply by dint of taking so many blows – and then finds booze. Poverty, the unfairness of life and

the cruelty of others see him sliding inexorably toward skid row. 'All a guy needed was a chance,' says Hank. 'Someone was always controlling who got a chance and who didn't.' *Ham on Rye* combines the fury, honesty and street poetry of Bukowki's earlier work with sad reflection and deep emotion. It brims with sharp observations of the trials of adolescence and working-class life: sexual yearning; the cruel and subtle hierarchies of the schoolyard; the mechanics of domestic abuse; the sadness of finally becoming stronger than one's father. But there are also moments of surprising tenderness: in one brief, beautiful early scene, Henry's father helps him feed sugar cubes to a horse. Towards the end, Henry's growing self-awareness is coupled with an understanding that he shares his despair with many others: his story is that of America's poor. Bukowski has two sides, the charismatic, witty barfly – a Tom Waits of literature – and the raving alcoholic, misanthropic and misogynistic. He truly lived the 'Beat' life Kerouac and others sought, but recognised, like his inspiration John Fante, how fierce and unforgiving that life could be. With *Ham on Rye*, Bukowski proved himself to be one of the greatest poets and chroniclers of America's dispossessed.

## 🕮Read on
*Post Office*; *Factotum*
John Fante, *Ask the Dust*; Henry Miller, *Tropic of Cancer*; Hubert Selby Jr., *Requiem for a Dream*

# WILLIAM S. BURROUGHS (1914–97)

## NAKED LUNCH (1959)

No one writes like William S. Burroughs – but then, how many other gay Midwestern, globetrotting, junky, (accidentally) wife-killing Beat writers are there? ›› Norman Mailer called him 'the only American writer who may conceivably be possessed by genius' and, alongside Burroughs' friend and editor Allen Ginsberg, testified at the 1965 Boston censorship court case to defend *Naked Lunch*. One of three central planks of Beat literature, alongside *On the Road* and *Howl*, *Naked Lunch* is actually closer to Ginsberg's priapic rant-poem than Kerouac's free-spirited novel. Plot and character take second place to ideas, presented in a consciously shocking series of vignettes. Central to the book is William Lee – the pseudonym Burroughs used for his first novel *Junky* – and *Naked Lunch* revisits locations frequented by the author, from New York to the drug-beds of Tangier and Mexico. Burroughs also invents hellish fictional locations, including the surreal Interzone, a nightmare version of the Tangier international zone enclosed in a 'single, vast building', with 'a hum of sex and commerce' and where everyone is 'queer' and 'available'. These worlds are populated by cold, unpleasant figures, among them the heroically evil psychological conditioner Dr Benway – who, when out of work, carries out alleyway abortions and prospects among heavily pregnant women – and the orgy-loving AJ. Less a novel than a series of cut-up fevered dreams, *Naked Lunch* is 'Jabberwocky' reinvented as twentieth-century nightmare. No wonder David Cronenberg adapted it (loosely) for the cinema: this is body horror *par excellence*, a torrent of sputum, sperm, excrement and vomit. It's astonishing to think this exactingly written festival of filth was penned in the 1950s. Yet like the writers he's influenced, J.G. Ballard in particular, Burroughs has purpose in his anarchic novel. He sees the commerce of junk dealing as representing American consumerism: 'Junk is the ideal product,' he wrote, attacking 'anti-drug hysteria'; he exposes the 'obscene, barbaric and disgusting anachronism' of capital punishment; but most of all, *Naked Lunch* is a diatribe against the social and psychological control he saw occurring in America. Burroughs may have seen the world differently to others, but perhaps his vision was, ultimately, truer than realism could ever be.

**Film version:** *Naked Lunch* (1991, directed by David Cronenberg and starring Peter Weller as Bill Lee)

## Read on

*The Soft Machine*; *Cities of the Red Night*
Kathy Acker, *Blood and Guts in High School*; ›› Jack Kerouac, *Visions of Cody*; ›› Chuck Palahniuk, *Choke*

## READONATHEME: ALTERED STATES (Drink and Drugs)

Nelson Algren, *The Man with the Golden Arm*
>> William S. Burroughs, *Junky*
>> Bret Easton Ellis, *Less Than Zero*
Frederick Exley, *A Fan's Notes*
Donald Goines, *Dopefiend*
Charles Jackson, *The Lost Weekend*
John O'Hara, *Appointment in Samarra*
Hunter S. Thompson, *The Rum Diary*

# TRUMAN CAPOTE (1924–84)

## BREAKFAST AT TIFFANY'S (1958)

Born in New Orleans and brought up in Alabama, Truman Capote began publishing short stories in magazines such as *Harper's Bazaar*, *Mademoiselle* and *The New Yorker* when he was in his early twenties. He went on to publish two novels (*Other Voices, Other Rooms* and *The Grass Harp*) before producing his most characteristic and best-known work of fiction, the novella *Breakfast at Tiffany's*, which first appeared in 1958 in a collection which also included three of his short stories.

This elegant and witty novella is the story of Holly Golightly, a young woman from Texas who has reinvented herself as a girl about town in New York. Seen through the eyes of the unnamed narrator, an aspiring writer who lives in her apartment block, Holly's life is a whirl of parties, night-clubs and dates with richer and older men but there are darker undercurrents swirling beneath the surface. There are plenty of reasons for the tears the narrator notices Holly shedding when she falls briefly asleep in his apartment. She has a long way to go to find a place that she can call home. Capote never truly fulfilled the promise of his twenties and thirties when ›› Norman Mailer called him 'the most perfect writer of my generation'. *In Cold Blood*, his 'non-fiction novel' about the real-life killing of a family in Kansas, is a remarkable work but too much of his talent in the last two decades of his life was dissipated in drink, drugs and squabbling with his society friends. The books that did appear during his long decline and after his death, such as *Music for Chameleons* and *Answered Prayers*, proved to be pale reflections of his earlier genius. However, *Breakfast at Tiffany's*, together with his other novellas and short stories from the 1950s, live on as the best memorials to a sparkling and wholly original writer.

◄**Film version:** *Breakfast at Tiffany's* (1961, starring Audrey Hepburn as Holly Golightly)

**≋Read on**
*In Cold Blood*; *Other Voices, Other Rooms*
Elaine Dundy, *The Dud Avocado*

# RAYMOND CARVER (1938–88)

## WHAT WE TALK ABOUT WHEN WE TALK ABOUT LOVE (1981)

Some guys may have all the luck but Raymond Carver wasn't one of them. His sawmill-worker father was a drunk, his mother a waitress. Though he worked blue-collar jobs while writing poetry and short stories, by his late twenties Carver was bankrupt and an alcoholic himself. Later, he wrote and taught his way out of manual work, but he died of cancer in 1988, aged only 50. Yet this tested man was also the most influential American short story writer of his generation. Blessed by a fruitful relationship with his editor, Gordon Lish, Carver's iconic work connects Hemingway's raw realism to the postmodernism of Auster – nowhere more beautifully than in the 1981 collection *What We Talk About When We Talk About Love*. Carver was not concerned with extraordinary cosmopolitan lives, but the moments of flux for everyday folk. His stories are modern fairytales in which the moral message and framing are removed, often to ominous or melancholy effect: in 'Tell the Women We're Going', it's the unexpected end to two men's chasing of girls; in 'So Much Water So Close To Home', it is the decision of four 'family men' on a fishing trip to delay reporting their discovery of a murdered woman. Other tales, meanwhile, make the everyday magical through withheld details, as in 'Why Don't You Dance?', in which a man dances with a couple In his furniture-filled yard. Carver's own life looms large in the stories. Drink and fatherhood come up repeatedly, often, as with all the expressions of love here, paired with inexpressiveness and misunderstanding: in 'Sacks', a father relates his affair to his grown-up son at an airport bar; in the title story, a gin-soaked discussion of love gains unexpected violence. Carver's instantly identifiable prose nails the rhythms of speech and how people tell stories to one another. His style is all-American: direct, unpretentious, widescreen even at the smallest level. His muscular minimalism is so dense with meaning that the gaps actually become the story, not unlike Carver's own life – and in the end, those gaps amount to a great deal.

## ≋Read on

*Cathedral*

>> Richard Ford, *Rock Springs*; Thom Jones, *The Pugilist at Rest*; Wells Tower, *Everything Ravaged, Everything Burned*; Tobias Wolff, *Our Story Begins*

# WILLA CATHER (1873–1947)

## MY ÁNTONIA (1918)

Willa Cather wrote idiosyncratic and impressive works of historical fiction (*Death Comes for the Archbishop* is a story of French Catholic missionaries to New Mexico) but the novels for which she is mostly known are set in the American Midwest she knew from her childhood, growing up in Nebraska at the end of the nineteenth century.

*O Pioneers!*, for example, is the story of a Swedish immigrant family, the Bergsons, and their struggles to make a living from their prairie farmstead. *My Ántonia* has a similar setting. Through the eyes of the narrator Jim Burden, the book tells the life story of Ántonia Shimerda, the eldest daughter of a family of immigrant farmers in Nebraska. Ántonia is a powerful personality – she 'had always been one to leave images in the mind that did not fade', according to Burden – and, in the course of the novel, her strength and determination to survive are severely tested. When she is still only a teenager, her father, homesick and unable to settle in his new country, commits suicide. Forced to work for others, she struggles to retain her independence and her sense of self-worth. As a young woman, an unhappy and ill-fated love affair leaves her with an illegitimate child and a tarnished reputation. Yet, when Burden, by now a successful city lawyer, returns after twenty years to visit the land he knew in his childhood, he finds that Ántonia has married a fellow immigrant and is at the centre of a large and happy family. Both a record of the determination with which spirited and hard-working immigrants opened up the prairies and an acknowledgement of how the harshly beautiful landscape shaped and restricted their lives, *My Ántonia* is the finest and, in many ways, most characteristic work of one of the greatest celebrants of American frontier values.

## ≋Read on
*Death Comes for the Archbishop*; *O Pioneers!*
Ellen Glasgow, *Barren Ground*; ≫ Edith Wharton, *Ethan Frome*

# MICHAEL CHABON (b. 1963)

## THE AMAZING ADVENTURES OF KAVALIER AND CLAY (2000)

Chabon was only twenty-five when he published his debut novel, *The Mysteries of Pittsburgh*. It became a bestseller and its success was such that Chabon, like many another writer, found it difficult to produce a second novel to match it. It was seven years before *Wonder Boys* was published and this turned out to be a quirky comedy about a writer finding it difficult to write a second novel to match his first. Chabon has since found much inspiration in genre and juvenile fiction, the themes and motifs of which he reworks for his own ends. *The Amazing Adventures of Kavalier and Clay*, for example, which won the Pulitzer Prize for Fiction and is perhaps his finest novel, makes use of comic book heroics in its story of two Jewish cousins who taste success in the Golden Age of Comics. Sammy Clayman is a young man living with his family in a small flat in New York, obsessed by comic books and dreaming 'the usual Brooklyn dreams of flight and transformation and escape'. His life is changed when his cousin Joe Kavalier arrives from Prague. Joe has left his country in the wake of the Nazi invasion but the rest of his family has been obliged to remain in Czechoslovakia. The two cousins join forces and, out of the amalgamation of their differing fantasies of freedom and power, they create a superhero named The Escapist, saviour of 'those who languish in tyranny's chains'. They persuade a publishing firm to back them and the comic book they produce becomes a huge success. Joe soon has money to spend and a lover, Rosa Saks, with whom to spend it but he cannot help his family back in Prague. When he does try to help them, the result is tragedy. Life is not like the comic books. *The Amazing Adventures of Kavalier and Clay* is a generous and endlessly inventive novel which explores both the potential of the imagination to rescue and redeem reality and the limitations it faces in that task.

⇘**Read on**
*Wonder Boys*; *The Yiddish Policemen's Union*
Glen David Gold, *Carter Beats the Devil*; ≫ Jonathan Lethem, *The Fortress of Solitude*

# RAYMOND CHANDLER (1888–1959)

## THE BIG SLEEP (1939)

Born in Chicago, Raymond Chandler actually spent his boyhood years living with his divorced mother in London and studying at Dulwich College – his famous creation Philip Marlowe is named after the school's Marlowe House. He returned to the USA as a young man in 1912 but it wasn't until 1933 – after he had fought in the war, written poetry, been fired as an oil man, drunk too much and had innumerable affairs – that he was first published in 'pulp' magazine *Black Mask*. And at the age of fifty in 1939, his first novel, *The Big Sleep*, confirmed Chandler to be a revelation. Its star is hard-drinking, taciturn private

detective Philip Marlowe, who exists in a Los Angeles where the women are no good and the men are worse. He is hired by elderly, wealthy General Sternwood to investigate a blackmail attempt relating to the gambling debts of one of his two wild daughters – but there's also the mystery of why her bootlegger husband disappeared. As Marlowe is drawn deeper into LA's sleazy underworld, the bodies begin to pile up …
Though **>>** Dashiell Hammett pioneered hardboiled, realistic crime fiction, Chandler's self-avowed literary sensibility was wholly new, *The Big Sleep* being the sleekest example of it. His instantly identifiable prose is full of colourful similes and metaphors; full stops riddle its staccato flow like bullet holes; the *noir* dialogue crackles with electric one-liners and sad poetry, such as 'Dead men are heavier than broken hearts'. Marlowe, meanwhile – who crucially maintains a strict moral code and is masterfully characterised in Chandler's witty first-person narration – is the model for every maverick crime and thriller hero from Michael Connelly's Harry Bosch and Ian Rankin's Rebus through to Lee Child's Jack Reacher. Chandler's Marlowe novels, starting with *The Big Sleep*, changed the way that America saw itself during and after the 'public enemy' era. It chimed with a nation that lapped up the real-life crimes of John Dillinger and Al Capone, it expressed what was happening on its mean streets – and that would only get worse as the century of guns and gangs wore on.

🎬**Film versions:** *The Big Sleep* (1946, starring Humphrey Bogart as Philip Marlowe); *The Big Sleep* (1978, starring Robert Mitchum as Philip Marlowe)

## ☙Read on

*Farewell, My Lovely*; *The Long Goodbye*

James M. Cain, *Double Indemnity*; ›› Dashiell Hammett, *The Maltese Falcon*; ›› James Ellroy, *The Black Dahlia*; Ross MacDonald, *The Drowning Pool*

---

## READONATHEME: DOWN THESE MEAN STREETS (The American Detective)

Lawrence Block, *A Dance at the Slaughterhouse*

James Lee Burke, *Cadillac Jukebox*

K.C. Constantine, *The Man Who Liked to Look at Himself*

Robert Crais, *The Monkey's Raincoat*

Loren D. Estleman, *Downriver*

Chester Himes, *A Rage in Harlem*

Jonathan Latimer, *The Lady in the Morgue*

Sara Paretsky, *Indemnity Only*

Robert B. Parker, *God Save the Child*

George P. Pelecanos, *A Firing Offense*

---

# JOHN CHEEVER (1912–82)

## THE WAPSHOT CHRONICLE (1957)

Often seen as the creator of placid suburban tales, John Cheever wrote work that hides a dark underbelly, mostly stemming from personal angst. Cheever knew that his shoemaker father had asked his mother for an abortion, and never shook the belief that he was a mistake; he also looked down upon his parents' struggling financial situation. He became a master of the short story who mixed with the right set – ›› Bellow, ›› Updike – married above his class and had three children, but behind closed doors he was a self-destructive alcoholic and closeted self-hating homosexual. Cheever found escape in his creations. His first full-length work, *The Wapshot Chronicle* (1957), is the story of Massachusetts brothers Moses and Coverly Wapshot and sings of his New England heritage. Their gentrified hometown is the ex-industrial port of St Botolphs, a place rich with fading tradition and populated by walking ghosts like their journal-writing ferryman father Leander. The arrival of rich, elderly Puritan Cousin Honora causes the brothers to leave to seek wives and new lives, but new beginnings come with endings. In its photo-album tone of melancholy, nostalgic distance, the novel resembles life glimpsed from a stopped train's window and related in exquisite, detailed and diversionary style. Yet in the Wapshots' emotional entanglements, life bursts forth in all its messy reality, from married Coverly's conflicted sexuality – echoing Cheever's demons – and Leander's poignant slide into irrelevance, to the mores of Moses' social climbing and Honora's fear of modern America's siege upon her family castle. The book finds great power as a reflection of

Cheever's self-loathing and loneliness. In one poetic passage Leander looks back at an evening when, after a young Coverly had seen *A Midsummer's Night's Dream*, he tried to fly like Oberon and crashed to the floor: 'He felt, standing above his naked son in the presence of something mysterious and unrestful – Icarus! Icarus! – as if the boy had fallen some great distance from his father's heart.' One feels that, though he kicked the drink and found literary acceptance, John Cheever never quite picked himself up off that floor.

**⮑Read on**
*The Collected Stories of John Cheever*; *Falconer*; *The Wapshot Scandal*
John O'Hara, *Appointment in Samarra*; ⟫ John Updike, *The Centaur*

# KATE CHOPIN (1851–1904)

## THE AWAKENING (1899)
Married at the age of twenty, Kate Chopin had six children by the time she was twenty-nine and it was only when she was widowed a few years later that she began to write seriously. Her short stories appeared in a variety of magazines in the 1890s, including *Vogue* and *Atlantic Monthly*, and she went on to publish two collections of them and two novels. Chopin's work was largely forgotten in the decades immediately

after her death but she has since come to be recognised as one of the most significant American writers of her era. The short novel entitled *The Awakening* is her best-known work. It tells the story of Edna Pontellier, a wife and mother living in some comfort in Louisiana who comes to question the life she is leading. During a summer vacation, her flirtation with the young and romantic Robert Lebrun awakens her to the idea that there may be more to life than social conventions suggest. On her return from vacation to New Orleans she determines to act upon her newly aroused feelings. Working as a painter and selling her paintings gives her a greater sense of independence and she asserts this further by moving out of the family home and engaging in a brief affair with a charming but egotistical womaniser. However, as Chopin's short narrative unfolds, Edna finds that the forces of conformity and convention are stronger than she believed and that she has been defeated in her attempts to escape them. *The Awakening* broke new ground in American fiction with its willingness to acknowledge female desire and its implicit argument that marriage and motherhood might not be all that women need to find self-fulfilment. Its ability to shock may have disappeared in the course of a century but its story of one woman's battle to enlarge her horizons remains moving and compelling reading.

📖 **Film version:** *Grand Isle* (1991, starring Kelly McGillis as Edna Pontellier)

📚 **Read on**
*At Fault* (Chopin's only other novel); *Bayou Folk* (short stories)
Charlotte Perkins Gilman, *The Yellow Wallpaper and Other Stories*;

Sarah Orne Jewett, *The Country of the Pointed Firs*; Elizabeth Stoddard, *The Morgesons*

# JAMES FENIMORE COOPER (1789–1851)

## THE LAST OF THE MOHICANS (1826)

The novels of James Fenimore Cooper, in which rugged pioneers battle against nature and potentially treacherous Indians to push the frontier forwards, were among the first to take specifically American subjects and present them to an audience both at home and abroad. More sophisticated writers have often made fun of his work (Mark Twain once joked that, 'In one place in *The Deerslayer* and in the restricted space of two-thirds of a page, Cooper scored 114 offences against literary art out of a possible 115') but his importance in the history of American fiction is difficult to deny. His themes and motifs and characters have been echoed in innumerable novels published in the century and a half since his death. His most famous work is *The Last of the Mohicans*. Set in the Seven Years' War of the 1750s, this tells the story of the white woodsman Natty Bumppo, also known as Hawkeye, and his Indian companions Chingachgook and Uncas, a father and son who are the last surviving members of a once-flourishing tribe. While hunting in the forest, the three men come across a small party travelling between two forts. The group includes Alice and Cora Munro, the daughters of the

British commander at Fort William Henry, and is being guided through dangerous territory by an Indian scout named Magua. This encounter is the beginning of a complicated narrative in which the young women are threatened by the treachery of Magua, and Hawkeye and his friends risk their lives (Uncas indeed loses his) in order to protect them. *The Last of the Mohicans* owed its original success to Cooper's ability to fashion an American story in the then newly-developed genre of historical fiction established in Europe by Sir Walter Scott. It has continued to attract readership and critical attention because of the ways in which it embodies nineteenth-century ideas about the frontier and, in its depiction of the doomed romance between Cora and Uncas, about race and sexuality. And, of course, because it remains, in part, a damn good adventure yarn.

**Film versions:** *The Last of the Mohicans* (1936, starring Randolph Scott as Hawkeye); *The Last of the Mohicans* (1992, starring Daniel Day-Lewis as Hawkeye)

**Read on**
*The Deerslayer* (the last of Cooper's 'Leatherstocking Tales' to be written but the earliest in chronology, set some dozen years before the events in *The Last of the Mohicans*); *The Pathfinder*
Owen Wister, *The Virginian*

# STEPHEN CRANE (1871–1900)

## THE RED BADGE OF COURAGE (1895)

Stephen Crane died of tuberculosis before he reached the age of thirty but, at the time of his death, he had already established himself as a major force in American fiction and he was much admired by writers as different as ➤➤ Henry James and Joseph Conrad. *The Red Badge of Courage* is the story for which he is best remembered. This short narrative focuses on Henry Fleming, a young soldier in the Union Army, who dreams of military glory but finds the reality very different from his dreams. An early encounter with the enemy ends in a mass, panicky retreat and Henry is so traumatised by fear that he himself turns and flees. Separated from his regiment, he wanders aimlessly behind the front lines, witnessing the chaos and confusion of warfare. He first chastises himself for what he sees as his cowardice in running and then persuades himself that his flight was justified because he survived to fight again. He joins a column of wounded men and, envying the 'red badge of courage' each one carries, he tries to hide the fact that he is unscathed. He watches one of the men die and can do nothing about it. Eventually, he stumbles across another band of soldiers in retreat and one of the men in flight strikes him with a rifle butt, gashing open his head. When Henry is reunited with his own regiment, his comrades believe he has been shot in battle. The following day, as battle recommences, he fights like a fury and carries the flag into the heat of the fray. The novel ends ambivalently with Henry feeling 'a quiet manhood' after his experiences but aware also that what he has passed through has been 'the red sickness of battle'. *The Red Badge of Courage* is one of the most extraordinary of all works of war literature, made even more remarkable by the fact that it was written by a man who, when he wrote it, had never personally experienced a battle at first hand.

**Film version:** *The Red Badge of Courage* (1951, directed by John Huston)

**Read on**
*Maggie: A Girl of the Streets*; *The Open Boat and Other Tales of Adventure* (short stories)
Frank Norris, *McTeague*; Michael Shaara, *The Killer Angels*

---

## READ ON A THEME: THE AMERICAN CIVIL WAR

Howard Bahr, *The Black Flower*
Russell Banks, *Cloudsplitter* (about John Brown and the Harper's Ferry raid)
James Lee Burke, *White Doves at Morning*
Shelby Foote, *Shiloh*
Charles Frazier, *Cold Mountain*
MacKinlay Kantor, *Andersonville*
>> Gore Vidal, *Lincoln*
Robert Penn Warren, *Wilderness*
Daniel Woodrell, *Woe to Live On* (filmed by Ang Lee as *Ride with the Devil*)
Stephen Wright, *The Amalgamation Polka*

# DON DeLILLO (b. 1936)

## UNDERWORLD (1997)

An Italian-American New Yorker born in 1936, Don DeLillo came from a family of typical first-generation immigrants and he was a typical boy, enjoying sports and playing in the Bronx streets. Later, a career in advertising gave way to literature and at least four genuine masterpieces – *White Noise* (1985), *Libra* (1988), *Mao II* (1991) and *Underworld* (1997) – that have defined postmodern fiction. *Underworld* was his eleventh novel, a Cold War narrative spanning forty years in which the death of one America – family-orientated, earthy, honest – is divided from the consumerist, individualistic present by one event: Russia's detonation of the atomic bomb. In an opening as memorable as any in American fiction, DeLillo locates us at the famous 1951 Dodgers-Giants baseball match, which climaxed with the home run known as 'The Shot Heard Round the World'. As young Cotter Martin escapes clutching the ball from the winning strike, another game attendee, J. Edgar Hoover, is informed that the Soviet Union has tested an atomic bomb. The subsequent narrative hops around chronologically and globally to show us money, waste and nuclear-induced paranoia ripping the heart out of America. Holding the narrative together is Bronx-raised Waste Containment worker Nick Shay, to whom the legendary baseball passes. Shay undergoes a series of personal detonations and consequent domestic fallout, culminating in the revelation of a terrible crime he committed in his youth. Though it can be overly sprawling and slow, *Underworld* is nevertheless as ambitious and meaningful as any American work of the past thirty years. It was a thunderclap, a shot heard around the world that influenced a generation of novelists and put DeLillo in the company of those earlier continent-straddling figures – ›› Mailer, ›› Bellow, ›› Roth and ›› Updike – who tried to define at an essential level what America is. In a final twist, the original cover pictured the Twin Towers vanishing into the clouds with a church silhouetted in the foreground. Initially signifying the dominance of consumerism over spiritualism, the co-existence of old and new, after 9/11 it found a second resonance – a second fracture in the heart of the American soul that DeLillo could not have predicted, but somehow prefigured.

### ☜Read on
*Libra*; *Mao II*; *White Noise*
›› John Dos Passos, *USA*; ›› Jonathan Franzen, *The Corrections*; ›› Thomas Pynchon, *Against the Day*

# PHILIP K. DICK (1928–82)

## THE MAN IN THE HIGH CASTLE (1962)
Literature and cinema have long been intertwined. In the case of the psychologically troubled Philip K. Dick, the tragedy is that the movie versions of his science-fiction novels came after his death at only fifty-three in 1982 – the same year that Ridley Scott's *Bladerunner* (based

on *Do Androids Dream of Electric Sheep?*) gained him the mainstream acceptance he'd yearned for and saw him being adapted for the movies at a rate surpassed only by ➤➤ Stephen King. Yet Dick's greatest novel, 1962's *The Man in the High Castle*, has never been filmed – perhaps it is too grimly *real* for Hollywood. It envisages a 1960s America in which Roosevelt was assassinated and the Axis powers won the Second World War, the country subsequently split between Japanese and Nazi empires. The action focuses on Japanese-ruled San Franciscans, including a US-memorabilia salesman, the rich men who buy his wares, and a forger of pre-war guns. Those serving under Japan find their rulers harsh but fair, and look towards the Reich with horror – most of all for its liquidation of Africa. Now, as mysterious industrialist Baynes says, 'The madmen are in power'. But German dissidents are on the move ... The term 'visionary' is overused, but Dick's Wellsian contemplation asks some severely troubling questions, such as how easily American culture fuses with that of the new world order: East Coast Americans dye their skin to look more Japanese; Jews undergo extensive surgery to look gentile; slavery is once more acceptable; Southern ethnic divides play into Nazi racism. Dick's story is more than an exceptional alternative history, however. In the title character, Hawthorne Abendsen, he finds his opposite, the author of an *I Ching*-influenced cult novel that imagines a world in which the Allies had won. Thus Dick's story refracts as much as it reflects, not only a *cri de coeur* against casual fascism, but for the importance of his art as a warning that history is created in the minds of those who live and write it. As Dick, America's amphetamine-popping tortured prophet, wrote in 1980: 'It's not just "What if" – it's "My God, what if" – in frenzy and hysteria.'

## ≋Read on

*Flow My Tears, the Policeman Said*; *The Three Stigmata of Palmer Eldritch*; *Ubik*

Alfred Bester, *The Demolished Man*; Thomas M. Disch, *Camp Concentration*; ›› Philip Roth, *The Plot Against America*

### READONATHEME: FUTURE AMERICAS AND ALTERNATIVE AMERICAS

Terry Bisson, *Fire on the Mountain*
›› Michael Chabon, *The Yiddish Policemen's Union*
›› Jack London, *The Iron Heel*
›› Cormac McCarthy, *The Road*
Ward Moore, *Bring the Jubilee*
›› Vladimir Nabokov, *Ada or Ardor: A Family Chronicle*
›› Walker Percy, *Love in the Ruins*
Norman Spinrad, *The Iron Dream*
George R. Stewart, *Earth Abides*
Jack Womack, *Elvissey*

# E.L. DOCTOROW (b. 1931)

## RAGTIME (1975)

Edgar Lawrence Doctorow was born in the Bronx, New York, the son of second-generation Americans of Russian-Jewish descent, and published his first novel, *Welcome to Hard Times*, an idiosyncratic version of a Western narrative, in 1960. He has since published more than a dozen other novels and volumes of short stories, including *Billy Bathgate*, the story of a fatherless teenager in the Bronx who becomes a surrogate son to the mobster Dutch Schulz, *The Waterworks*, a tale of corruption, child abuse and a mad search for immortality in 1870s New York, and *The March*, set during General Sherman's march through Georgia and the Carolinas in the last days of the American Civil War. The best known and most widely admired of his works, however, is *Ragtime*, in which fictional characters and real individuals from early twentieth-century American history meet and interact on the page. A family of Doctorow's invention, unnamed except in generic terms as Father, Mother and Mother's Younger Brother, leads a life of upper middle-class ease in the town of New Rochelle. An immigrant and his young daughter, newly arrived in the country, experience the worst hardships of poverty and the violence of industrial disputes before the father chances upon the path to prosperity. Coalhouse Walker, a black pianist based on a character from a classic German novel, is propelled into violence by prejudice, injustice and his own refusal to compromise his principles. Meanwhile the beautiful Evelyn Nesbit finds herself at the heart of the most scandalous murder case of the era when her husband Harry Thaw shoots her former lover, the architect Stanford White, the escapologist Harry Houdini enthrals the nation with his daring stunts and J.P. Morgan and Henry Ford meet to discuss the destiny of mankind. In fitting together all these disparate characters and the stories they have to tell, Doctorow produced a rich and rewarding literary mosaic.

**Film version:** *Ragtime* (1981, directed by Milos Forman)

**Read on**
*Billy Bathgate*; *The March*; *The Waterworks*
Kevin Baker, *Dreamland*; >> Gore Vidal, *Empire*

# JOHN DOS PASSOS (1896–1970)

## MANHATTAN TRANSFER (1925)

Like other American writers of his generation (>> Hemingway and E.E. Cummings, for example), Dos Passos found the First World War, in which he served as an ambulance man, an experience which entirely altered his perception of the world. His earliest success as a novelist came with the publication in 1921 of *Three Soldiers*, a deliberately unheroic and realistic account of three men from very different backgrounds who serve in the US army during the Great War. *Manhattan Transfer* followed four years later. It was immediately seen as a work of great significance. Sinclair Lewis, then at the height of his fame and soon to become the first American writer to win the Nobel Prize for Literature, declared that it 'may be the foundation of a whole new school of novel-writing'. Through a series of overlapping stories – of Jimmy Herf, a wealthy young man turned radical journalist, of Gus McNeil, a working man who wins money in a lawsuit after he is knocked down by a train car and uses it to launch himself as a politician, of George Baldwin, a lawyer who becomes McNeil's rival, of Ellen Thatcher, an actress who is loved by both Herf and Baldwin – Dos Passos gradually builds up a fictional mosaic of the life of New York which is unlike any other account of the city. He went on to extend the narrative experimentation that he pioneered in *Manhattan Transfer* in his trilogy, *USA*, which makes use of stories, collages of newspaper clippings and the ephemera of popular culture, short biographies of prominent people and a stream-of-consciousness autobiography to create a vast panorama of American life in the first few decades of the twentieth century. Dos Passos is one of the most unjustly neglected of great American writers of the twentieth century and *Manhattan Transfer* provides the ideal introduction to his fascinating and demanding work.

## ☜Read on

*Adventures of a Young Man*; *Three Soldiers*; *USA* (the trilogy consists of three volumes, originally published separately and entitled *The 42nd Parallel*, *Nineteen Nineteen* and *The Big Money*)
E.E. Cummings, *The Enormous Room*; ❯❯ Ernest Hemingway, *The Sun Also Rises*

# THEODORE DREISER (1871–1945)

## AN AMERICAN TRAGEDY (1925)

Born in Indiana, the son of a German immigrant to the state, Dreiser began his career as a journalist and published his first novel, *Sister Carrie*, in 1900. This story, controversial in its day, of a young woman rising from rags to riches in the theatre while her middle-aged lover moves inexorably in the opposite direction, was a pioneering work of American literary naturalism. Dreiser followed it with a number of other novels which turned a jaundiced eye on American society and its extremes of wealth and poverty but his finest work is probably *An American Tragedy*. Loosely based on a notorious murder case which had fascinated him twenty years earlier, the novel tells the story of Clyde Griffiths, a young man with ambitions who sees them threatened when he gets a girl pregnant. As Dreiser's novel begins, Clyde is a disaffected teenager embarrassed by the poverty and piety of his parents, devout Christians who insist on his joining them in their missionary work in the more wretched streets of Kansas City. He turns away from their example in search of a more exciting, fulfilling and (most importantly) financially rewarding life. First as a bellboy in a hotel and later as the foreman of a factory in New York State owned by his uncle, he reaches out for worldly success. He yearns for marriage with Sondra Finchley, the daughter of a wealthy friend of his uncle, but he seduces Roberta Alden, a girl working at the factory. When Roberta announces that she is pregnant, Clyde can see only one way out of the dilemma in which he finds himself. Dreiser is not, by any stretch of the imagination, American fiction's greatest stylist and his prose is often criticised as lumpen and laborious but

*An American Tragedy* is a book that rises above its limitations to become a powerful and dark indictment of the American Dream.

### ⮑Read on
*Sister Carrie*; *Jennie Gerhardt*
John O'Hara, *Appointment in Samarra*; Booth Tarkington, *The Magnificent Ambersons*

# DAVE EGGERS (b. 1970)

## YOU SHALL KNOW OUR VELOCITY (2002)
A socially and culturally active writer brought up in suburban Chicago, as the founder of Brooklyn publishing house *McSweeney's* and its ultra-fashionable literary journal of the same name, Dave Eggers is currently one of the most influential authors in America. Possessed of a restlessly creative mind, Eggers made his debut with *A Heartbreaking Work of Staggering Genius* – published when he was 29 – a semi-fictionalised account of his bringing up of his younger brother after the premature deaths of their parents. Eggers' first novel *You Shall Know Our Velocity* is a more abstract and less emotional book that asks one question: how easy is it to fly around the world in a week and get rid of $38,000? That's the issue plaguing Will and his fact-loving friend Hand, after the death of their friend Jack and a beating-up Will suffers. They set

off on a haphazard, ridiculous quest to fritter away the money by whatever means possible, from burying it to trying to tape it to a goat. The means by which Will comes by the money – his silhouette is used on light-bulb branding – satirises that variety of American ambition that regards monetary gain as success, coming through no skill but also bestowing no pleasure. Their self-concerned travels also sends up the disinterested box-ticking American tourism that resides mostly in airports; yet despite Will's final epiphany on this score, the (occasionally annoying) pair are really on the run from genuine grief. There is an inherent sweetness to Eggers' writing: this is a man who loves people, as evidenced by his community work and his very human Hurricane Katrina book *Zeitoun*. The novel has postmodern pizzazz too: photos and visual devices; blank pages representing a boat flying through the air; Will's humorous imagined conversations – this is a post-cinema novel that reads like a Sundance Festival indie film meeting the atomised structure of *On The Road*. It also represents a neat summation of Eggers' essence: a serious concern for the fate of individuals twinned with ebullient, magical storytelling. The story may be slight, but it proves that Eggers possesses the best play box in the literary world today.

## ⮂Read on
*A Heartbreaking Work of Staggering Genius* (memoir); *How We Are Hungry* (short stories); *What is the What*
Joshua Ferris, *The Unnamed*; ›› Jonathan Lethem, *Chronic City*; ›› David Foster Wallace, *The Broom of the System*

# BRET EASTON ELLIS (b. 1964)

## AMERICAN PSYCHO (1991)

It begins with a quote from Dante's *Inferno* ('Abandon all hope ye who enter here') and sure enough, every sin imaginable is practised in *American Psycho*. From an unremarkable background in Los Angeles, Bret Easton Ellis created himself as a literary provocateur and fashionista: he got published by the age of twenty-one with *Less Than Zero*, moved to New York, hung out with authors like ›› Jay McInerney, and was openly ambiguous in his sexuality. But most importantly, in 1991 his third book *American Psycho* was published to the greatest literary furore since *The Satanic Verses*. Its star is Wall Street yuppie Patrick Bateman, who exists in a world where you are what you do. He compares business cards with colleagues; he talks money, fashion and smooth music; he snorts blizzards of cocaine. But he is also a brutal, sexually depraved serial killer. And as his murderous side bleeds into his daily life, reality itself becomes fuzzy and Bateman's sense of self is brought into question. An uncompromising novel in every way, far from being the shallow sex and drug-fest that contemporary reactions might have suggested, *American Psycho* resembles the 'Theatre of Cruelty' of Antonin Artaud. Linguistically, it leaves nothing unsaid: there is no line that cannot be crossed, its throbbing present-tense description hammering home the impact. But put in the context of his other work, it also proves Easton Ellis to be a vital force who can employ all the tricks of modern writing – from metafictional self-reflexive narrative to stream of consciousness – to create something genuinely new. Yes, *American Psycho* is a vicious satire about 1980s greed, but it's also a study of the annihilation of the self. In this respect, it achieves greatness not by being specifically tied to the 1980s, but by fitting into that realm of self-destructive hedonism – the clash of Nietzschean will to power with the insane idealism of the capitalist dream – explored in ➤➤ Charles Bukowski's *Post Office*. And at the end, when everything shocking that can be said has been said, there simply stands a broken man. That is the novel's lasting triumph.

◀**Film version:** *American Psycho* (2000, starring Christian Bale as Patrick Bateman)

⊗**Read on**
*Glamorama*; *Less Than Zero*; *Lunar Park*
➤➤ Charles Bukowski, *Post Office*; Dennis Cooper, *Frisk*; ➤➤ Chuck Palahniuk, *Fight Club*; ➤➤ Tom Wolfe, *The Bonfire of the Vanities*

# RALPH ELLISON (1914–94)

## INVISIBLE MAN (1952)
'I am a man of substance, of flesh and bone, fiber and liquids – and I might even be said to possess a mind,' the unnamed, African-American protagonist of Ralph Ellison's groundbreaking first novel states in the book's prologue, 'I am invisible, understand, simply because people

refuse to see me.' The novel follows its central character's journey from a small town in the Deep South, where he suffers at the hands of the local whites but eventually wins a scholarship to an all-black college, to the streets of New York. Expelled from college after a series of mis-adventures while escorting one of its white trustees around town end in a fight in a bar, the 'invisible man' heads for the city but can find no employment save in menial jobs. Even these prove the gateway to further humiliations. He is obliged to spend time as a mental patient. His attempts to further the cause of social justice and his membership of a left-wing group known as 'The Brotherhood' show only how unfraternal those who proclaim the unity of mankind can be. Ellison's anti-hero is left to contemplate his continuing invisibility, the ways in which those who deal with him 'see only my surroundings, themselves, or figments of their imagination – indeed, everything and anything except me'. More than simply a novel about the black man struggling to survive in an unchangingly white world, *Invisible Man* is a powerful novel for all those who have, at some time, felt excluded or ignored. In other words, for just about everybody. Ellison worked for decades on a second novel, *Juneteenth*, but it remained unfinished (at least to his own satisfaction) at the end of his life. It has since appeared in a version edited by his biographer and literary executor John F. Callahan. His first novel stands alone as the solitary but towering achievement of his literary career.

## ⩪Read on

*Juneteenth*

James Weldon Johnson, *The Autobiography of an Ex-Colored Man*; ››
Richard Wright, *Native Son*

# JAMES ELLROY (b. 1948)

## THE BLACK DAHLIA (1987)

*Noir* to the bone, James Ellroy is today's foremost proponent of hardboiled crime as originated by ›› Hammett, Cain and Chandler. Like ›› Chandler, Los Angeles is his infernal muse, the city in which he was born in 1948 into a family divided, while his bleak worldview is often ascribed to the murder of his mother in 1958 – a case that, like the real-life murder of Elizabeth Short portrayed in *The Black Dahlia*, went unsolved. He dedicated the book to his mother; indeed, with typically bare honesty, Ellroy has admitted to glibly using his mother's murder to publicise the book. But the emotion born of that tragedy – which caused the young Ellroy to become lost in drugs, drink, petty crime, voyeurism and Nazi dalliances – makes the history breathe. It's January 1947. America is booming, LA a glittering modern metropolis. Then young, beautiful Betty Short is brutally murdered and mutilated. The first cops on the scene are Bucky Bleichert and Lee Blanchard: ex-boxers, best friends and in love with the same woman. Lee is hooked on the case; Bucky dragged in against his will. The media go crazy, the public become luridly fascinated with the sexual violence of the crime. And when Bucky sleeps with a bisexual woman connected to the victim, a sordid obsession with the Dahlia breeds in him as corruption within and without blossoms. Narrated by Bucky, Ellroy's sparse to-the-point description is pitiless and raw. The voice of the novel's ambitious, egotistic and unapologetically right-wing author is right there – the rot, he's telling us, was in America from the start, the sickness in people from birth. But there too is the utterly authentic voice of the LAPD in all its slangy, locomotive propulsion. *The Black Dahlia* is more alive and more shocking than any period piece has a right to be, perhaps because of Ellroy's own psycho-sexual issues, perhaps because Bucky's dark obsession opens his most personal wound. Ellroy gets the degradation of the seedy hoi polloi like no one else because he's been there and back, he's both sides of LA's grimy coin, for as Bucky says: 'The good guys were really the bad guys'.

**Film version:** *The Black Dahlia* (2006, directed by Brian De Palma)

**Read on**
*The Big Nowhere*; *LA Confidential*; *White Jazz* (the other three volumes in the LA Quartet); *American Tabloid*
Michael Connelly, *The Black Echo*; Joseph Wambaugh, *The Choirboys*

# LOUISE ERDRICH (b. 1954)

## LOVE MEDICINE (1984)
Born in Minnesota and brought up in North Dakota, where her parents worked for the Bureau of Indian Affairs, Louis Erdrich has drawn on the riches of her Native American, more specifically Chippewa, heritage to create a body of work that includes several volumes of poetry, books for children and more than a dozen novels. Many of Erdrich's novels have

been set in North Dakota where she has constructed her own fictional landscape, sometimes compared to ▶▶ William Faulkner's Yoknapatawpha County, in which to locate the lives and stories of the characters she has created. Her sense of the land and how it shapes the lives of those who inhabit it was apparent from her very first novel, *Love Medicine*, published originally in 1984 but thoroughly revised and expanded a decade later. This is a collection of interlocking stories which unfold over more than a half century and three generations of a group of families living on an Indian Reservation in North Dakota. The focus of the book is provided by a love triangle involving Nector Kashpaw, married to Marie Lazarre, but long the lover of Lulu Nanapush who bears him a child he cannot bring himself to acknowledge. Readers are first introduced to them when they are young in the 1930s and they are still to the fore in what is the pivotal story in the book, the one which provides it with a title. In the chapter entitled 'Love Medicine', Lipsha Morissey, a young man with the gift of healing is recruited by his grandmother Marie to distract Nector, now an old man wandering in his mind, from his continuing obsession with Lulu. Filled with a variety of voices, each helping to build up a rich mosaic of stories, memories and myths, *Love Medicine* marked the arrival of someone ▶▶ Philip Roth called, 'the most interesting American novelist to have appeared in years'.

## ☙Read on

*The Beet Queen*; *Tracks*
Paula Gunn Allen, *The Woman Who Owned the Shadows*; N. Scott Momaday, *House Made of Dawn*; Leslie Marmon Silko, *Ceremony*

# JEFFREY EUGENIDES (b. 1960)

## THE VIRGIN SUICIDES (1993)

Jeffrey Eugenides was forty-three when he won the Pulitzer Prize in 2003 for *Middlesex*, the sweeping story of his home city's rise and fall told by a truly memorable Greek immigrant narrator. In many ways it is the archetypal Great American Novel, but his 1993 debut *The Virgin Suicides* achieves something just as profound: the exposing of suburban America's broken heart. Down a middle-class tree-lined street, behind a white picket fence, the bland, smothering Lisbon household is disintegrating. Looking back on the events of their childhood, a group of men remember the summer that all five Lisbon girls committed suicide, starting with peculiar Cecelia, clothed in a wedding dress. To these narrators, who talk in the collective 'we' – as in Joshua Ferris's *Then We Came To The End* – these were halcyon high-school days when teens were 'distraught at hands of love'. They were, and are, almost fetishistically fascinated by the mystical 'Other' of the Lisbon girls, especially sexually active Lux, yet respect for them is negligible, even in death – they are bras and body parts, as much a collective as the boys doing the narrating. These unsympathetic narrators are the young 'Me generation' who, as they admit, have been cosseted by their parents' lies: 'Occasionally we heard gunshots coming from the ghetto, but our fathers insisted it was only cars backfiring.' To them the year of the suicides was a simpler, magical time, glowing with the 'pale ghosts of fish flies' and bonfires 'blazing orange'. Like ❯❯ Shirley Jackson and ❯❯ Stephen King, Eugenides is strong on the small-mindedness of suburbia. Of the youths' snobbery, some is standard high-school hierarchicalism, some crueller, such as the narrators' disgust with 'Joe the Retard'. This is learned from their parents, whose behaviour ranges from petty bitchiness about leaves on the lawn to explicit racism, while public interest in the suicides oscillates between heartless flippancy and macabre preoccupation. Eugenides's portrayal of the way that this closed society deals with, exploits and even enjoys the suicides – while rejecting any form of difference – is troubling, shocking, darkly funny and often moving.

**Film version:** *The Virgin Suicides* (1999, directed by Sofia Coppola)

**Read on**
*Middlesex*
>> Shirley Jackson, *The Lottery and Other Stories*; Jhumpa Lahiri, *The Namesake*; >> Donna Tartt, *The Secret History*

# WILLIAM FAULKNER (1897–1962)

## THE SOUND AND THE FURY (1929)
William Faulkner was as influential as Samuel Beckett, Virginia Woolf or >> Hemingway in introducing a new form of artistic language: in Faulkner's case, spiralling, digressive storytelling infused with Southern Gothic and impressionistic stream-of-consciousness. Encouraged by

Sherwood Anderson to pursue fiction over poetry, he produced a decade-long run of classics with the South as his canvas, beginning in 1929 with *The Sound and the Fury*. It eventually won him a Nobel Prize in 1949. Dense, difficult and with an almost otherworldly power derived from its fractured viewpoints and shattered chronology, *The Sound and the Fury* is still shocking today, its truths leaping out of its highly subjective narratives like jack-in-a-boxes. The book explores the disintegration of the rich, white Compson family in the rural South in the decades up to April 1928, and revolves around three brothers' obsession with their sweet-hearted, sexually wild sister Caddy. Innocent, mentally disabled thirty-three-year-old Benjy, who is utterly devoted to caring Caddy, tells the remarkable first chapter in simplistic but confused form as experiences in the present trigger aching flashbacks of his past with her. Damaged Harvard student Quentin takes us back to the day of his suicide in 1910 as he yearns troublingly for his sister; bitter money-driven monster Jason rants and raves in the third part. In the fourth, an omniscient narrator blows away the fog to reveal what Benjy tried to tell us. As a game-changing modernist text that explores subjectivity as both a literary style and our means of knowing, *The Sound and the Fury* demonstrates the elusiveness both of individuals and of an objectively understandable 'truth'. Crucially, however, it's also a breath-haltingly emotional take on moral decrepitude, family pride, racial tension and fiercely destructive love in the post-Civil War, pre-civil rights South, just as its values and heritage were crumbling. Read it fast, and Faulkner's headlong tumble into the Compsons' minds is a rush of received memory and upending horrors, like a Greek tragedy lived from the inside; read it slow, and the book offers up a whole new way of telling stories that finds poetry in existentialism.

**⬛Film version:** *The Sound and the Fury* (1959, starring Yul Brynner and Joanne Woodward)

**📖Read on**
*Intruder in the Dust*; *Light in August*
≫ Ralph Ellison, *Invisible Man*; ≫ Cormac McCarthy, *Suttree*; William Styron, *Lie Down in Darkness*

# F. SCOTT FITZGERALD (1896–1940)

## THE GREAT GATSBY (1925)

Amongst claimants to the title of 'Great American Novel' one brief book towers above all others: F. Scott Fitzgerald's *The Great Gatsby*. Born in St Paul, Minnesota in 1896, its author wrote from an early age, through his Princeton years and a brief stint in the army. He married his beloved Zelda a couple of years later – their tempestuous relationship is reflected in his most famous novel – and they moved to New York, home of what he coined the 'Jazz Age', into which the revered writer leaped with an alcohol-misted, lavish-living abandon that was to undo him in years to come. *The Great Gatsby* is a stirring evocation of that freeing social whirl, but the book has fathomless depths beyond the surface glamour of the all-night parties Gatsby throws in his opulent mansion. Its narrator is Nick Carraway, a strait-laced middle-class young man who, having fled his Midwest upbringing, lives in 'slender riotous'

Long Island's posh West Egg village, New York. He hangs out with the more fashionable types, including brash, wealthy Tom Buchanan and his wife Daisy, a distant relative. Then their world is cracked open when he meets his neighbour, the mysterious social god Jay Gatsby, whose whole affluent, gregarious persona is a self-created myth behind which he can pursue his once-lost love: Daisy. Gatsby, relentlessly fascinating both to us and to his celebrity party guests, exposes America's love of the rich enigma, from Howard Hughes to Elvis. In his poverty-stricken past and self-made, fragile present, he both represents and demolishes the American Dream: here heartache and despair cannot be dodged by reinvention; illusion and disillusion go hand in hand. Fitzgerald's genius is to cram a dreamily evocative social satire and devastating love story into one volume of extraordinarily delicate language and emotion. As intoxicating as a highball sipped at sunset on a perfect lawn, as heartbreaking as a stumbled-upon letter from a former lover wafted with perfume, *The Great Gatsby* is more than the greatest novel of the Jazz Age: it's timeless.

**Film versions:** *The Great Gatsby* (1949, starring Alan Ladd as Gatsby); *The Great Gatsby* (1974, starring Robert Redford as Gatsby)

## Read on
*The Beautiful and the Damned*; *Tender is the Night*
>> Ernest Hemingway, *The Sun Also Rises*; >> Dawn Powell, *A Time to Be Born*

# JONATHAN SAFRAN FOER (b. 1977)

## EVERYTHING IS ILLUMINATED (2002)

Young Brooklyn-based novelist Jonathan Safran Foer is part of the new wave of trendy American fiction writers that emerged at the turn of the twenty-first century. Brought up in a middle-class Jewish family in Washington DC, he studied philosophy at Princeton, where ›› Joyce Carol Oates also tutored him in creative writing. His thesis for this course became the basis of his 2002 debut novel, *Everything Is Illuminated*. The story follows his fictionalised search for the woman who saved his grandfather from the Nazis during the war but the narrative is far from straightforward and is told in three interrelated threads. The first is Safran Foer's fragmentary, Marquez-like retelling of his family's history in a Ukrainian *shtetl*; the second covers the search itself, told in clumsy English by the vulgar, ego-driven Alex, who serves as Safran Foer's guide alongside his grumpy grandfather and an amorous dog called Sammy Davis, Junior, Junior; the final thread comprises Alex's letters to Safran Foer about the developing manuscripts. Safran Foer brings together the three threads with deftness and empathy to create a fresh exploration of Jewish-American identity filtered through a tricksy metafiction. Though the self-conscious conceits initially threaten to overwhelm the book, Safran Foer's writing – full of humorous absurdity, crudity and touching pathos – allows it to blossom into something truly original. Like the writing of ›› Dave Eggers, Safran Foer's work is a direct and vibrant descendant of cutting-edge American writing: the absurdist humour recalls ›› Vonnegut; he writes himself into his novel like ›› Paul Auster; he plays with the very form of type and layout in a tradition that stretches back at least as far as ➤➤ Dos Passos. But most of all Safran Foer is not afraid to be daring in his approach to big subjects – the Holocaust in *Everything Is Illuminated* or 9/11 in his second book, *Extremely Loud and Incredibly Close*. Though Safran Foer's detractors criticise his copious and self-conscious employment of fashionable literary devices, it is this joy in the art of storytelling and the printed word as a physical artform that see him in better shape to adapt to the future of publishing than most other writers.

### ➤Read on

*Extremely Loud and Incredibly Close*
➤➤ Dave Eggers, *A Heartbreaking Work of Staggering Genius*; James Frey, *A Million Little Pieces*

# RICHARD FORD (b. 1944)

## THE SPORTSWRITER (1986)

Richard Ford is usually associated with the loose and ill-defined literary movement that was given the name of 'dirty realism' in the 1980s. Indeed he was editor of several of the collections of short stories which provided dirty realism with what little focus it had as a movement. Yet Ford always made an unlikely candidate for inclusion in the group. He was no 'laureate of the dispossessed' like ➤➤ Raymond Carver, the most

famous exponent of dirty realism. He was always more of a celebrant of
the ordinary pains and pleasures of relatively affluent and middle-class
people like Frank Bascombe, the protagonist of Ford's most
characteristic novel, and the first which brought him to wider attention,
*The Sportswriter*. Some time before the weekend in 1983 on which the
novel is set, Frank suffered the devastating loss of his young son who
died of a little-understood childhood disease. He has divorced his wife
but he is refusing steadfastly to stare into the abyss. Indeed, he copes
with his bereavement by ignoring it as much as possible and focusing
instead on the everyday demands of his job. He admires the sports
heroes of whom he writes and yearns for the kind of grace under
pressure that he believes they possess. In contrast to them, he seems
to drift through life, dreamily detached from it. The novel focuses on an
Easter weekend and the events in it (a visit with his ex-wife to his son's
grave, a dinner with his current girlfriend's family) but continually
moves backwards through Frank's memories to the time of his marriage
and his bereavement. In the course of the weekend, Ford's
unobtrusively skilful plotting nudges his protagonist towards a new
sense of himself and his life. Making the ordinary seem compelling,
even heroic, in a novel is no easy task but it is one that Ford achieves
with elegance and grace in *The Sportswriter*.

## ⮧Read on

*Independence Day*; *The Lay of the Land* (two sequels to *The
Sportswriter*); *Rock Springs* (short stories)
>> Raymond Carver, *Cathedral*; Jayne Anne Phillips, *Machine Dreams*;
>> Anne Tyler, *The Accidental Tourist*

# JONATHAN FRANZEN (b. 1959)

## THE CORRECTIONS (2001)

As a child in suburban Webster Groves, Missouri, Jonathan Franzen was a nerdy boy who, according to his book *The Discomfort Zone*, was afraid of most social activity and his parents most of all. His wildly successful (and hyped) third novel, *The Corrections*, wows by affixing those neuroses to skilled micro-observation; ironically it propelled him into the arms of the New York literati. The book orbits around the Midwestern Lambert family, headed by stern Parkinson's-afflicted Alfred and his fussing, anxiously optimistic wife Enid. She is attempting to bring her three children back west for 'one last Christmas' in St Jude. They are: financially incompetent ex-professor Chip, fired for sleeping with a student; high-flying, sexually-driven chef Denise; and depressed banker Gary, who's increasingly estranged from his wife and sons. But first this dysfunctional family must overcome infidelities, financial crimes and deep-seated resentments. *The Corrections* is a stunning feat of empathetic characterisation. From tiny interpersonal skirmishes Franzen extrapolates out to create a whole universe of interconnected existences whose emotional equilibrium is constantly out. Alfred Lambert is a superb creation, his past as a capable, masculine railwayman juxtaposing sadly with the senile, lost old man whose only stab at independence is owning a chair relegated to the basement; Franzen's father died from Alzheimer's, and he writes incredibly movingly about dementia. His own small-town upbringing translates into a poetically written evocation of the Midwest: the gentle passing of time, the fall of leaves and light, the slow-developing attitudes. The only misstep is an unconvincing section in which Chip, muddled up with gangsters, travels to post-Soviet Lithuania. Published in 2001, *The Corrections* pinpointed the national issues of identity and morality that surfaced in the post-9/11 Bush years, especially the clash of the traditionalist Midwest with the intellectual, liberal Northeast. Franzen can be hilarious one moment and poignant the next, springing from Chip's dire screenplay or the mores of cruise ship life to the brutalising effect of consumer culture on the old. In exploring our search for permanence and relevance in the modern world *The Corrections* resurrected classic storytelling for a new millennium – and there can be no higher praise than that.

### ☙Read on
*The Twenty-Seventh City*; *Strong Motion* (Franzen's two earlier novels)
>> Jeffrey Eugenides, *Middlesex*; Joshua Ferris, *Then We Came to the End*

# WILLIAM GIBSON (b. 1948)

## NEUROMANCER (1984)
William Gibson was born into the science-fiction golden age. He grew up in first Virginia then Arizona until, as a bookish, William S. Burroughs-loving young man, Gibson lost both his parents and dodged

the draft by heading to Canada in the 1960s. His landmark 1984 novel *Neuromancer* recognised the fledgling World Wide Web as a game-changer and ran with it, changing the course of science fiction and winning all the major genre awards. Its hero is 'console cowboy' and drug addict Case, a washed-up computer hacker. Exiled from 'the matrix' – a digital reality built on a global network – he wanders the dystopian 'neon forest' of Chiba, Japan, addled by neural damage and in hock to gangsters. Lured by a physically augmented 'street samurai' called Molly, Case accepts treatment from ex-military man Armitage, but winds up tricked into planning an attack for him on an icy super-AI called Wintermute. Like the finest *noir*, *Neuromancer* is awash in Cold War paranoia, but where once the setting would have been bombed-out Berlin, here we get a Japanese megalopolis in which the poor sleep in 'coffins', a gasoline-and-limestone Istanbul and an American super-city called the Sprawl (recalling ›› Burroughs' Interzone). The book teems with remarkable images: holograms boxing in a grimy bar; air swelled into a bass throb by a silent train; 'faint neon molecules crawling beneath the skin'. But it's the vividness of Gibson's virtual reality and the downhill sensation of the real world's dissolution that amazes in a world when genetic engineering and pharmaceuticals have rendered the body no more than 'meat'. The fringes of the digital frontier make for a compelling narrative environment, realised in a nightmarish post-punk aesthetic that saw Gibson crowned the creator of 'cyberpunk' (a term he invented). There are a handful of science-fiction novels that reconfigured the way we think about the infrastructure of the world we live in: *Brave New World*, *Nineteen Eighty-Four* and *Neuromancer*. While as a literary achievement it doesn't scale the heights of either Huxley's or Orwell's work (the characters, in particular, disappoint), as an oracle-like peer down the dark digital rabbit hole it is near flawless.

### ☙Read on
*Virtual Light*; *Pattern Recognition*
>> William S. Burroughs, *Nova Express*; >> Philip K. Dick, *Do Androids Dream of Electric Sheep?*; Neal Stephenson, *Snow Crash*

# DASHIELL HAMMETT (1894–1961)

## THE GLASS KEY (1931)
A former private detective himself, Dashiell Hammett turned to writing stories and serials for the pulp magazines in the 1920s and later became a Hollywood scriptwriter. The crime fiction he produced in the dozen years from the appearance of his first 'Continental Op' short story in 1922 to the publication of his last novel, *The Thin Man*, in 1934 revolutionised the genre. He added realism to a kind of fiction which had hitherto seemed to have only a distant relationship to the real world. In the words of >> Raymond Chandler, Hammett 'gave murder back to the kind of people that commit it for reasons, not just to provide a corpse; and with the means at hand, not hand-wrought duelling pistols, curare and tropical fish'. His best-known work is probably *The*

*Maltese Falcon*, familiar from a memorable 1940s film version starring Humphrey Bogart. However, his finest novel may well be *The Glass Key*, an unflinching portrait of gangsterism and city politics, in which a tarnished anti-hero, Ned Beaumont, negotiates his way through a maze of deceit and corruption. Set in an anonymous American city near New York, the novel focuses on Beaumont and his friend Paul Madvig, a crooked political wheeler-and-dealer who is working to ensure that his man, Taylor Henry, is re-elected to the Senate. However, when Henry's son is murdered, suspicion falls on Madvig and Beaumont sets out to unearth the truth. Is one of the politician's many enemies trying to frame him? Or is there another reason for the killing? Ned Beaumont's quest is complicated by his growing attraction to Taylor Henry's daughter, who just happens to be Madvig's fiancée, and by his boss's battle with a mobster named Shad O'Rory. Told in the crispest and sharpest of prose, *The Glass Key* is Hammett's darkest vision of crime, corruption and American politics.

**Film version:** *The Glass Key* (1942, starring Alan Ladd as Beaumont)

**Read on**
*The Maltese Falcon*; *Red Harvest*
James M. Cain, *The Postman Always Rings Twice*; ➤➤ Raymond Chandler, *Farewell, My Lovely*; Raoul Whitfield, *Green Ice*

# NATHANIEL HAWTHORNE (1804–64)

## THE SCARLET LETTER (1850)

A member of a long-established New England family, Hawthorne was born in Salem, Massachusetts – the town in which the notorious witch-trials of the seventeenth century had taken place – and much of his work is concerned with his heritage of New England Puritanism. He wrote and published fiction throughout his adult life but his greatest achievements belong to an extraordinary burst of creativity in the late 1840s and early 1850s, which saw the publication of *The House of the Seven Gables*, *The Blithedale Romance* and, most importantly of all, *The Scarlet Letter*. Set in seventeenth-century Boston, this novel has as its central character a young woman named Hester Prynne. When the main narrative opens, she faces the wrath of the Puritans in her community who pillory her and brand her as an adulteress, making her wear the scarlet letter A embroidered on her clothes. Two years earlier, Hester had travelled from England ahead of her elderly husband and, when he failed to arrive in the New World, seemingly lost at sea, she took a lover and became pregnant. Now she refuses to name her lover and she and her child, Pearl, become outcasts in the community. A man calling himself Roger Chillingworth, in reality Hester's missing husband, arrives in Boston in time to witness her disgrace and he vows to discover the identity of the lover and have his revenge. His suspicion falls on the Reverend Arthur Dimmesdale and, as the years pass, he worms his way into the minister's household and adds additional torments to the guilt and remorse that Dimmesdale is already suffering. While Hester redeems her 'sin' by living a virtuous and Christian life, her husband and her lover pursue a bitter enmity which damages both themselves and nearly everyone with whom they come into contact. Through their story, Hawthorne explores and criticises the ideas of sin and guilt and expiation which he saw as permeating the American culture in which he lived.

📽**Film versions:** *The Scarlet Letter* (1995, starring Demi Moore as Hester Prynne, Gary Oldman as Dimmesdale and Robert Duvall as Chillingworth)

📖**Read on**
*The Blithedale Romance*; *The House of the Seven Gables*
**>>** Edgar Allan Poe, *Tales of Mystery and Imagination*; **>>** Herman Melville, *The Confidence Man*

# JOSEPH HELLER (1923–99)

## CATCH-22 (1961)

The madness of war has never been better captured than in the pages of Joseph Heller's dazzlingly comic first novel about a group of US bomber pilots stationed on a Mediterranean island during the Second World War. At its heart is the paradox that gives the book its title. Every time a man thinks he has flown his quota of bombing missions, high command doubles the number. There is no escape, and the reason is

Catch-22: if you're sane enough to ask to be grounded because what you're doing is crazy, you're sane enough to fly. If you're crazy enough to fly the missions, you don't have to but as soon as you ask to be grounded that proves you're no longer crazy and you do. 'That's some catch, that Catch-22,' remarks Yossarian, the anti-hero of Heller's world turned upside down. 'It's the best there is,' he is told. Around the figure of Yossarian, 'the crazy bastard' who may be 'the only sane one left', circles a rich array of memorable characters. There is Milo Minderbinder, the lunatic entrepreneur who takes the freedom of the market to such wild extremes that he ends by signing contracts for bombing missions with the Germans and arranging for the dropping of explosives on his own base. There is Major Major Major, a man condemned to ridicule by the convergence of his name and his army rank. There is Colonel Cathcart, the wildly ambitious commander of the base, who looks upon Yossarian as the bane of his life. None of Heller's later books achieved quite the success of *Catch-22* which remains one of the greatest American novels of the second half of the twentieth century. As the writer himself once remarked, 'People say that, in the last thirty years, I haven't written a novel as good as *Catch-22*. True, but, then, nor has anyone else.' In *Catch-22*, he looks at the horrors of war and invites us to laugh uproariously in the dark.

**Film version:** *Catch-22* (1970, starring Alan Arkin as Yossarian)

## Read on
*Closing Time* (a sequel to *Catch-22*, in which Yossarian and his ex-comrades are facing old age, despair and death in 1990s New York); *Good as Gold*; *Something Happened*

>> Norman Mailer, *The Naked and the Dead*; >> Kurt Vonnegut, *Slaughterhouse Five*

# ERNEST HEMINGWAY (1899–1961)

## A FAREWELL TO ARMS (1929)

There is some fine fiction in the work Hemingway wrote in his middle and later years, after he had transformed himself into the macho figure of legend, swilling drink and shooting animals as he careered around the world in search of wars to witness and bullfights to attend. His 1940 novel *For Whom the Bell Tolls*, the story of an American discovering love and comradeship amidst the fighting in the Spanish Civil War, remains one of the best fictional depictions of that conflict. *The Old Man and the Sea*, published in 1951, is a wonderful account of an elemental struggle between an ageing fisherman and a giant marlin. However, for the best of Hemingway, it is necessary to look out the books he wrote as a young man. It is often difficult today to appreciate just how refreshing and unusual his spare and minimalist prose seemed in the 1920s and 1930s. His work exemplified a new honesty and directness in American fiction and *A Farewell to Arms*, perhaps more than any of his other novels, is representative of those early days. Frederic Henry is an American ambulance driver in Italy during the last years of the First World War who meets with a young English nurse,

Catherine Barkley. They embark on a playful game of love in which neither of them invests too much emotion but, when Frederic is wounded and Catherine becomes his carer, their feelings intensify. She becomes pregnant. Frederic, now recovered, must return to the Front where he experiences the chaos and misery of the Italian retreat from Caporetto. Utterly disgusted by the madness and violence of war, he deserts and he and Catherine flee to neutral Switzerland. Happiness seems to beckon for both of them but fate has a cruel trick up its sleeve. Poignant and moving in its simplicity and lack of pretension, *A Farewell to Arms* shows clearly why Hemingway was one of the great innovatory writers of the twentieth century.

**Film version:** *A Farewell to Arms* (1957, starring Rock Hudson and Jennifer Jones as Frederic and Catherine)

### Read on
*For Whom the Bell Tolls*; *The Old Man and the Sea*
>> John Dos Passos, *Three Soldiers*; >> F. Scott Fitzgerald, *This Side of Paradise*

# PATRICIA HIGHSMITH (1921–95)

## THE TALENTED MR RIPLEY (1955)

The defining figure in the life of Texan-born Patricia Highsmith was her hyper-critical mother, with whom she shared a vicious love-hate relationship. In adulthood Highsmith became a hard-drinking, bisexual misanthrope whose outspoken unpleasant views (including virulent racism) made her unpopular. Yet Highsmith's literary explorations of the perversion, cruelty and psychological abnormalities that fascinated her have far outlasted that personal image, especially her five Tom Ripley novels, starting with *The Talented Mr Ripley*. Ostensibly poor, schizophrenic and gay, Tom Ripley is a talented mimic and forger, skills he uses to make friends based on lies and to run small con jobs. In a bar he runs into Herbert Greenleaf, a shipping magnate who (mostly incorrectly) remembers him as being a friend of his errant playboy son Dickie, who is gallivanting around southern Italy with a woman called Marge. Tom is sent after Dickie, all-expenses paid, with the aim of bringing him home. In the picturesque village of Mongibello the shy yet creepily charming Tom manages to ingratiate himself with Dickie, but his dark impulses are soon hard to contain. A sensitive aesthete with no moral compass, Tom Ripley is one of the most complex characters in modern literature; he's also Highsmith's psyche writ large, a hollow ball of self-loathing filled with terrifying narcissism, misogyny and snobbery (her enmity for her home country emerges in Tom's hatred of the Americans invading his European idyll). Yet by a miraculous sleight-of-hand Highsmith makes Tom a sympathetic figure whose disturbed mind we anxiously come to relate to. An actor without a real identity, he kills to seek 'annihilation of his past and of himself' and, like a child deprived of parental love (as was Highsmith), to gain an audience and self-affirming love. Dickie is the object of that love, whom Tom envies 'with a heartbreaking surge of envy and self-pity'. Beyond being an acutely refined examination of sociopathy, *The Talented Mr Ripley* is also a relentlessly gripping thriller of law-avoidance and risk-courting: Graham Greene accurately called Highsmith 'a poet of apprehension'. In rooting for Ripley's fragile existence she makes us question who we really are ... and what we're capable of.

**Film versions:** *Plein Soleil* (1960, French adaptation starring Alain Delon as Ripley); *The Talented Mr Ripley* (1999, starring Matt Damon as Ripley)

**Read on**
*Ripley Under Ground*; *Strangers on a Train* (Highsmith's first novel, made into a memorable film by Alfred Hitchcock)
Margaret Millar, *Beast in View*; Jim Thompson, *The Killer Inside Me*

# ZORA NEALE HURSTON (1891–1960)

## THEIR EYES WERE WATCHING GOD (1937)

Zora Neale Hurston was one of the major figures in the 'Harlem Renaissance', that remarkable outburst of black creativity and artistic expression in Jazz Age New York which also brought writers such as Langston Hughes, Claude McKay and Jean Toomer to the nation's attention. Her short stories appeared in the landmark anthology of 1925, *The New Negro*, and her first novels were published in the 1930s. *Their Eyes Were Watching God* is set in Florida, the state in which Hurston had been brought up, and tells the story of Janie Crawford who has just arrived back in the black town of Eatonville after a long absence. She is looked upon with disapproval by many of the people in town and the novel takes the shape of the story of her life Janie tells to Pheoby, one of the few friends prepared to accept her. Raised by her grandmother, who grew up in slavery, Janie is married off at an early age to a man named Logan Killicks but it is another man, Joe Starks, who first stirs her sexually. She runs off with Joe to Eatonville where he becomes a big man about town but, over the years, he begins to treat Janie with contempt. When Joe dies, Janie's refusal to mourn hypocritically and her willingness to take up with a younger man named Tea Cake outrage the townsfolk of Eatonville. She and Tea Cake move away but tragedy awaits them in their new life. And yet, as she now explains to Pheoby, she can not regret her time with Tea Cake. No less a writer than ›› Alice Walker said of *Their Eyes Were Watching God* that 'there is no book more important to me than this one'. It tells a story of resilience, survival and the creation of an independent self and it tells it in a voice of unforgettable strength.

🐛**Read on**
*Dust Tracks on a Road* (autobiography); *Jonah's Gourd Vine*
Maya Angelou, *I Know Why the Caged Bird Sings* (the first volume of
Angelou's autobiography); Jean Toomer, *Cane*; **»** Alice Walker, *The
Third Life of Grange Copeland*

# JOHN IRVING (b. 1942)

## THE WORLD ACCORDING TO GARP (1978)

Born in 1942 in New England, John Irving uses the places and people of
his life as a foundation for his tales of sexual intrigue, parental issues
and artistic endeavour. In the National Book Award-winning *The World
According to Garp*, he stitched together these threads into a lush
tragicomic tapestry about one man's lifetime. Like Irving, who never
met his pilot father, T.S. Garp is raised only by his 'lone wolf' mother,
Jenny Fields. She is appalled by the idea of male-reliant 'lust' – in a
grimly comic scene, Garp is conceived when she rapes a comatose
soldier. Garp shares Irving's passions – wrestling, sex and writing – and
it is via the last of these that he wins the heart of the wrestling coach's
stunning, studious daughter Helen, with whom he fathers three
children. But life is full of bumps and cracks: Jenny's autobiography puts
her in harm's way when she becomes a feminist icon, while sexual
misdemeanours and bizarre tragedies threaten Garp's brittle marriage.
Few novelists are as adept as Irving at recreating real life's comedy and

heartbreak – like all of his expansive novels, and recalling nineteenth-century authors like Dickens and ›› Melville, *Garp*'s plot often feels like part of a wider story glimpsed via digressions and autobiographical details, including snatches of Garp's own increasingly bleak fiction. Irving also explores feminism without being didactic: Jenny's views are co-opted by radical activists, clashing with being a devoted mother; Garp deals with marital adulteries as well as powerful paternal anxieties. It's in the gaps between the extremes of their roles that life finds space for absurdism and tragedy. This fourth of Irving's books is the most gloriously imaginative of his reworkings of his life. Garp's stories echo not only his fictional life, but also Irving's past works – these realities slot together like Russian dolls to form one very human grand narrative about him, us and our reflections on each other, implicating the reader in the fatalistic, sometimes comedic horrors of the tale. As Irving's famous final line puts it: 'In the world according to Garp, we are all terminal cases'.

**◢Film version:** *The World According to Garp* (1982, starring Robin Williams as Garp)

## ❧Read on
*The Cider House Rules*; *A Prayer for Owen Meany*
Howard Norman, *The Museum Guard*; Tom Robbins, *Even Cowgirls Get the Blues*

# WASHINGTON IRVING (1783–1859)

## THE SKETCH BOOK OF GEOFFREY CRAYON, GENT.
(1819/1820)

Washington Irving was one of the first American writers to attract significant acclaim not only within the United States but also in England and the rest of Europe. Writing in the persona of Geoffrey Crayon, an erudite American traveller visiting the Old World, he produced a volume which mixed together stories and digressive essays to create a work that has charmed readers around the world for the best part of two centuries. *The Sketch Book of Geoffrey Crayon, Gent.* actually includes few pieces that could be described unequivocally as fiction and even fewer that have an American setting. Many of the sketches are rose-tinted evocations of a rural England that was already disappearing when Irving was writing. One of the few short stories in the book ('The Spectre Bridegroom') claims to be a tale told by a traveller in a Flemish inn and takes place in a version of Germany that owes more to Gothic literature than it does to reality. However, *The Sketch Book* justifies its place in a guide to the American novel because it contains two of the most familiar characters in American fiction. In 'Rip Van Winkle' Irving tells the story of its eponymous hero, a henpecked husband who wanders into the Catskill Mountains, meets a group of strangely dressed men playing ninepins, falls asleep after sharing a drink with them and only awakes twenty years later. Wandering back into his village, he finds that his wife is dead and that the War of Independence has rendered his expressions of loyalty to King George deeply suspicious to his neighbours. In 'The Legend of Sleepy Hollow', Ichabod

Crane is a schoolmaster in a New England township whose courtship of Katrina van Tassel comes to nothing when he encounters a supposed ghost known as the 'Headless Horseman' and disappears from the neighbourhood. Both stories won immediate fame and have long since established a permanent place in the collective American imagination, retold for each new generation and regularly reinvented in the cinema and on the TV.

**Film versions:** *The Legend of Sleepy Hollow* (1949, Disney cartoon film); *Sleepy Hollow* (1999, directed by Tim Burton and starring Johnny Depp as Ichabod Crane, this bears only a very slight resemblance to the original Irving story)

**Read on**
*Tales of a Traveller* (another similar collection of sketches and stories)
>> Nathaniel Hawthorne, *Twice-Told Tales*

# SHIRLEY JACKSON (1919–65)

## WE HAVE ALWAYS LIVED IN THE CASTLE (1962)
A subversive novelist and prolific short story writer throughout the 1940s and 1950s, Shirley Jackson wrote disturbing tales of evil behind the white picket fence which predate >> Stephen King's suburban Gothic horror and expose the class division and disunity in post-war

America. While her short stories in the *New Yorker* made her a well-read, if controversial name – most of all for 'The Lottery', whose shocking scenes of ritual small-town murder prompted hundreds of complaints to the magazine – Jackson herself struggled with everyday life. She succumbed to alcoholism, amphetamines and morbid obesity at the age of just forty-nine, shortly after the publication of *We Have Always Lived in the Castle*. Although *The Haunting of Hill House* is her best-known novel, it is this final book that is the purest expression of her sensibility. Its story introduces us to the Blackwood family, all but three of whom were poisoned six years ago, apparently by the agoraphobic, sweetly timid Constance. Together with senile Uncle Julian, and our narrator, the ritualistic, bitter younger sister Merricat, they live in seclusion in their manor house, away from a village that fears and resents them. Events spin out of control following the arrival of a distant cousin, exposing the dark heart of the Blackwoods' history – but perhaps an even darker side to the villagers' attitudes to the family. Just as ❯❯ Edgar Allan Poe used his own fear of being buried alive in his fiction, Jackson's growing agoraphobia towards the end of her life is brought into frightening solidity in the book. And like the Blackwoods, Jackson and her flamboyant Jewish literary critic husband were ostracised from their small hometown community in North Bennington, Vermont. Her voice comes through in her anti-heroine Merricat, one of the great unreliable narrators of American fiction, whose damaged mind fights to control the world around it. In *We Have Always Lived in the Castle* a terrifying portrait of the small-mindedness of suburban America is twinned with a timeless sense of Gothic horror. The book is a *Frankenstein* for the Cold War era in which the monster lives in society as well as within the soul.

**≋Read on**

*The Haunting of Hill House*; *The Lottery and Other Stories*
≫ Henry James, *The Turn of the Screw*; ≫ Stephen King, *Carrie*

# HENRY JAMES (1843–1916)

## THE PORTRAIT OF A LADY (1881)

Henry James was born and brought up in New England but settled in London in the 1870s and eventually became a naturalised British citizen the year before his death. In the course of his career, he wrote dozens of short stories, a number of novellas (including most famously *The Turn of the Screw*, a ghost story about two children haunted by a sinister figure named Peter Quint) and more than twenty novels. James's great subject as a writer was the meeting and mingling of the two cultures of the old world and the new and it was one which he explored in fiction that ranged from *Daisy Miller*, a short work focusing on a beautiful young American girl visiting Europe for the first time, to *The Ambassadors*, a long, ironical novel about how Europe changes a group of Americans, young and middle-aged, rich and poor, friends and strangers. However, none of his novels embodies his central subject better than *The Portrait of a Lady*. The lady in question is Isabel Archer, a young woman from New England who is brought to Europe by her aunt. After the death of her uncle, a retired banker who provides for her in his will, Isabel becomes a wealthy woman. Her inheritance excites the attention of Gilbert Osmond, a selfish and cynical aesthete in search of a way to marry into money. Aided and abetted by his long-term mistress, Madame Merle, Osmond exercises his charm on Isabel and they eventually become husband and wife. The marriage is doomed from the start by Osmond's egotism and lack of any real feelings for Isabel and, in a sequence of devastating revelations, she is forced to face the fact that, despite the independent spirit on which she has always prided herself, she has been duped by the scheming of Osmond and Madame Merle.

**Film version:** *The Portrait of a Lady* (1996, directed by Jane Campion and starring Nicole Kidman as Isabel Archer)

**Read on**
*The Ambassadors*; *The Bostonians*; *The Wings of the Dove*
William Dean Howells, *The Rise of Silas Lapham*; ›› Edith Wharton, *The Custom of the Country*

# JACK KEROUAC (1922–69)

## ON THE ROAD (1957)

Jack Kerouac came from French-Canadian stock and enjoyed a comfortable middle-class upbringing in Massachusetts, earning a scholarship to Columbia University. But he was also a restless soul: he dropped out, tried sports journalism, joined the navy and was thrown out after only a month. Yet from the moment *On the Road* was published in 1957, Kerouac's largely autobiographical second novel became part of a sweeping change in American culture: like Elvis Presley and James Dean, he brought sex, drugs and youthful abandon into the public and artistic realm. It's probably apocryphal that Kerouac wrote the book on one long benzedrine binge, but the book's story is true: its characters are pseudonyms for real figures (including Allen Ginsberg and ›› William S. Burroughs), with Kerouac at the centre as Sal Paradise and his friend Neal Cassady re-embodied as the paragon of 'beat' life, Dean Moriarty. To be 'beat' was to reject the accepted societal route to happiness and to seek something more real – in *On the Road*, that reality is life on America's highways. The book climbs on board Sal's car-mad journeys across the belt of America, with Dean leading the way to the next party, speeding onwards like a booze-fuelled devil. The writing is breathless, thrilling, poetic, occasionally straining too hard at the linguistic leash. There is little in the way of a strict narrative structure but then, that's the point: each crossing of the great continent is an irresistible search for the next buzz and a bigger high in a hunt for the 'real' America. Like ›› Philip Roth's *American Pastoral* and ›› Don DeLillo's *Underworld*, *On the Road* is a novel that seeks to define America by what it has lost: the ramshackle, brutal, live-for-today existences of a rural and urban working-class that Dean and his coterie emulate through their aimless, increasingly criminal wanderings. In their eventual flight into the heart of darkness that is Mexico, they finally find the real America as it once was: poverty stricken, exploitative and dangerous. Far from a eulogy of the American Dream, *On the Road* sets out a countercultural critique of all that has been lost on the road to modernity. True to his dark vision, Kerouac died before he was fifty, a victim of alcoholism: the road had run out.

### ≋Read on
*The Dharma Bums*
>> William S. Burroughs, *Naked Lunch*; John Clellon Holmes, *Go* (first published in 1952 and often described as the first 'beat' novel); Hunter S. Thompson, *Fear and Loathing in Las Vegas*

# KEN KESEY (1935–2001)

## ONE FLEW OVER THE CUCKOO'S NEST (1962)

In 1959, Ken Kesey, then a creative writing student at Stanford University, volunteered to act as a guinea pig in a series of medical trials into the effects of psychoactive drugs like LSD and mescaline. The experiences he had during these trials fed into the novel he was writing and the result was *One Flew Over the Cuckoo's Nest*. Set in a mental hospital in Oregon, the book is narrated by 'Chief' Bromden, a giant

American Indian who is a patient there. It tells the story of what happens to the other inmates of the hospital when the drugged routine of their lives is disrupted by the arrival of Randle McMurphy, a larger-than-life prankster who challenges all the rules and assumptions of the establishment. Faced by the petty and humiliating controls imposed on the male patients by the formidable Nurse Ratched, McMurphy noisily asserts his own individuality and struggles to persuade his fellow inmates that there is a life outside the hospital walls which they can still seize and enjoy. He leads them on a fishing expedition that gives them a new sense of their own possibilities; he smuggles booze and women into the ward for a night-long bacchanal that ends in tragedy. McMurphy is eventually defeated by the powers he sets out to confront but not before he has inspired his fellow patients and given 'Chief' Bromden the incentive to rediscover his true self and escape the hospital. Kesey's novel has its faults – it is overly if unapologetically romantic in its portrait of McMurphy and there is more than a hint of misogyny lurking behind the character and his defiance of Nurse Ratched – but *One Flew Over the Cuckoo's Nest* remains an unforget-table protest against all those forces in American society which conspire to regiment and restrict the human spirit.

**Film version:** *One Flew Over the Cuckoo's Nest* (1975, directed by Milos Forman and starring Jack Nicholson as McMurphy)

**Read on**
*Sometimes a Great Notion*
Edward Abbey, *The Monkey Wrench Gang*; ▶ Tom Wolfe, *The Electric*

*Kool-Aid Acid Test* (non-fiction account of Ken Kesey's adventures in the 1960s travelling across America with a group of like-minded spirits known as the Merry Pranksters)

# STEPHEN KING (b. 1947)

## CARRIE (1974)

Books have long obsessed over our fear of the 'Other', whether through the social realism of *Silas Marner* (on epilepsy) or the magical horror of *Frankenstein*. Multi-award-winning bestseller Stephen King combined these two approaches for his first published novel, *Carrie*. Initially planned as a short story to make a few bucks for his family, it is a fearful take on high-school life that has terrible resonance today. King based his novel on two high-school girls he knew, one a bullied schoolgirl who committed suicide and a second who struggled with epilepsy and a religiously fervent mother. Carrie White, his 'bovine' telekinetic seventeen-year-old from Chamberlain, Maine, is an amalgam of both, a tender reflection of the abuse American teens face at the hands of their peers and their families. Carrie's mother is a self-loathing Christian zealot; other girls have singled her daughter out for the bottom of the pile. Central to the relentless bullying is the demonisation (and self-demonisation) of women, recalling the supernatural mass hysteria of the Salem witch trials. In the upsetting opening prefiguring the prom-night climax, *Carrie* is traumatised when her period arrives (her mother having left her ignorant of the 'sin' of menstruation) in the gym showers. The girls taunt her; her mother beats her and shuts her in a cupboard. King is brilliant on the subsequent guilt of figures such as Carrie's groomed antithesis Susan Snell or well-meaning teacher Miss Desjardin – and how their good intentions are swept aside by their social systems. Like Dickens, King has the ability to hook with every word; he's the fireside horror-story teller turned professional writer. Here his storytelling is expanded by newspaper clippings and psychiatric reports. But *Carrie* is also touching, King giving his heroine the power to fight back denied those two real girls. To ban *Carrie* in schools, as in some states, seems self-defeating: these events already occur, and the echo of Columbine – another crime committed by outsiders – is inescapable by the end: 'It is not enough, these days, to say that Chamberlain will never be the same. It may be closer to the truth to say that Chamberlain will simply never again be.'

**Film version:** *Carrie* (1976)

**Read on**

*Misery*; *Pet Sematary*; *The Shining*

>> Ray Bradbury, *Something Wicked This Way Comes*; Ira Levin, *Rosemary's Baby*; Richard Matheson, *I Am Legend*; Peter Straub, *Ghost Story*

# BARBARA KINGSOLVER (b. 1955)

## THE POISONWOOD BIBLE (1998)

Like the great nineteenth-century novelists, Barbara Kingsolver believes that fiction has a duty to engage with the real world. She has even sponsored a prize, the Bellwether Prize, which is awarded to a first novel that combines both literary quality and a willingness to address issues of social justice. Her own novels, which she began publishing in the late 1980s, are old-fashioned in the best sense of the word. They grapple with the political, social and moral issues that affect us all. Her finest and most ambitious work is *The Poisonwood Bible* which tells the story of Nathan Price, a narrow-minded Christian evangelist, who arrives with his family in the Belgian Congo to serve as a missionary to African people to whom his message means little. The year is 1959 and great changes are on hand in the country. Independence from colonial rule has arrived but Belgian rule is about to be replaced by American interference. The first elected prime minister, Patrice Lumumba, is assassinated and replaced in a CIA-sponsored coup. However, the messianic Price is as blind to these political developments as he is to the real needs of his family and the people he has volunteered to 'save'. Kingsolver's story is told in the very different voices of Price's wife and his four daughters – pouting would-be prom queen Rachel, Leah (at first her father's greatest supporter but soon his fiercest critic), her twin sister Adah who suffers from hemiplegia but has her own idiosyncratic perspective on events, and five-year-old Ruth May. A series of personal tragedies unfolds amid the wider tragedy of a new nation still in thrall to the forces of economic imperialism. 'The writing of fiction,' Barbara

Kingsolver once wrote, 'is a dance between truth and invention.' *The Poisonwood Bible* is the most remarkable dance she has so far choreographed.

### ≷Read on

*The Bean Trees*; *Pigs in Heaven* (two linked novels, published before *The Poisonwood Bible*); *The Lacuna*
>> Jeffrey Eugenides, *Middlesex*; >> Jane Smiley, *A Thousand Acres*

# JERZY KOSINSKI (1933–91)

## BEING THERE (1971)

As a Jewish child in Poland, Jerzy Kosinski survived the Holocaust, but was separated from his parents. Later, he carved out an acclaimed career in academia and writing, drawing the attention of the repressive Soviet state. Like Nabokov, Kosinski found creative freedom in America, becoming a citizen in 1965, as well as a literary star with his first novel *The Painted Bird*, supposedly based on his traumatised childhood wanderings. The work most informed by Kosinski's American life, however, is *Being There*, a taut little satire that still speaks volumes today. Its central figure is Chance, a gardener bound to his elderly employer's estate whose only knowledge is of gardening and what he's gleaned from watching television. When the old man dies, Chance stumbles out into the world, where utterances like 'For everything there is a season' are misconstrued as metaphorical wisdom and make him a worldwide celebrity. Renamed Chauncey Gardiner via a linguistic misunderstanding, this wide-eyed man without an identity rises through the business ranks towards government. In a world today in which E! is watched by millions and Geri Halliwell is a UN ambassador, Chance is a more perfect modern hero than even Kosinski could have anticipated, reflecting the media's language back on itself in meaningless soundbites. And on an individual level, when he meets wealthy Elizabeth Eve 'EE' Rand, he wins her loyalty simply by 'repeating to her parts of her own sentences'. *Being There* continues to reflect a society in which people in power want to hear only flattery and platitude. Jerzy Kosinski played fast and loose with the truth about himself (even his name was assumed) and he was as much a self-creation as Jay Gatsby or Bob Dylan. Crises and contradictions followed him throughout his life. There were claims that he had invented much of the supposedly autobiographical material on which he said *The Painted Bird* was based and he was accused of plagiarising the idea for *Being There* from a Polish novel of the 1930s. In 1991, aged fifty seven, Kosinski killed himself. *The New York Times* reported that the night before 'he appeared cheerful and gregarious at a crowded book party' – but then, perhaps that's just what people wanted to see.

📖**Film version:** *Being There* (1979, starring Peter Sellers as Chance)

📖**Read on**
*The Painted Bird* (set in Poland during the Second World War)

James Frey, *Bright Shiny Morning*; ➤➤ Vladimir Nabokov, *Pnin* ➤➤ Kurt Vonnegut, *Cat's Cradle*

# HARPER LEE (b. 1926)

## TO KILL A MOCKINGBIRD (1960)

If the most resonant novels are written in times of change, then *To Kill a Mockingbird* rings doubly loud. Harper Lee's Pulitzer Prize-winning book of 1960 is a coruscating, knife-sharp story of racism in America's Deep South in the 1930s. The author herself (a descendant of Robert E. Lee) was writing about what she knew. The daughter of an Alabama lawyer, she was born in 1926 (and was therefore the same age as its heroine Scout in the year in which it is set) and she pours her experiences into this remarkable novel. With great subtlety and warmth, the book's first half draws us into the sleepy rural Alabama community of Maycomb and the relationships of the Finch family. It is narrated by tomboy Scout (really Jean Louise), who describes life with her young brother Jem in their motherless household, run by idealistic state defence lawyer Atticus. Into their idyllic childhood intrudes the ugly truth of a racially divided society, as Atticus takes on the defence of Tom Robinson, a black man accused of raping a lower-class white woman. Early on, Lee's foreboding images have a lyrical simplicity: a snowman built of mud is coated in white snow; a rabid dog is shot in the street by

Atticus because he is the only man who can do the job; as the brother and sister are given air rifles, Atticus tells them 'it's a sin to kill a mockingbird'. As the rape trial begins, we see the children's loss of innocence and the flourishing of their empathetic skills, brought to life in Scout's utterly convincing narration. Childish fears about Boo Radley – the mysterious neighbourhood bogeyman who never leaves his home – transmute into real fears about racial hatred. If *The Great Gatsby* chronicles the seismic changes of interwar society, *To Kill a Mockingbird* is about older, Civil War-era divisions. Here is the America of *Huckleberry Finn* half a century later, yet essentially unchanged. At a time when America has its first black President, we can look back on *To Kill a Mockingbird* to see how far we've come – or how little.

◀**Film version:** *To Kill a Mockingbird* (1962, starring Gregory Peck as Atticus Finch)

📖**Read on**
➤➤ William Faulkner, *As I Lay Dying*; Ernest J. Gaines, *A Lesson Before Dying*; Hillary Jordan, *Mudbound*; ➤➤ Mark Twain, *The Adventures of Huckleberry Finn*

## READ ON A THEME: SMALL TOWN AMERICA

Sherwood Anderson, *Winesburg, Ohio*
Fannie Flagg, *Fried Green Tomatoes at the Whistle Stop Café*
Kent Haruf, *Plainsong*
Garrison Keillor, *Lake Wobegon Days*
Larry McMurtry, *The Last Picture Show*
Sinclair Lewis, *Main Street*
Elizabeth Strout, *Olive Kitteridge*
Adriana Trigiani, *Big Stone Gap*
>> Anne Tyler, *The Tin Can Tree*
James Wilcox, *Modern Baptists*

# URSULA K. LE GUIN (b. 1929)

## THE LEFT HAND OF DARKNESS (1969)

Only the very best science-fiction writers achieve widespread literary acclaim. Ursula K. Le Guin is one of them. Author of the much-loved *Earthsea* fantasy series for children, as well as numerous short stories, poetry collections and essays, she stands alongside Margaret Atwood as the genre's most respected female practitioner. Le Guin's science-fiction novel, *The Left Hand of Darkness*, was the start of a string of books that helped transform cultural approaches to futuristic writing and made her the first female winner of the Hugo award. Like Atwood's *The Handmaid's Tale*, the book brings gender politics into stark relief in what the author described as a 'thought experiment'. It concerns Genly Ai, an envoy for a vast, multi-planet-spanning human collective called the Ekumen, and his attempts to persuade the mutually antipathetic Karhide and Orgoreyn countries of the ice planet Winter to join it. Crucially, the people of Winter are asexual hermaphrodites, except once each month during the 'kemmer', when they become either male or female to mate. We see Winter through Ai's eyes, a stranger alone 'in the heart of the Ice Age of an alien world'. Misunderstandings and mistrust shape his relationships with the planet's inhabitants, due largely to his stereotyping of gender roles, but his tender and growing friendship with the Karhide prime minister Estraven – the emotional core of the book – eventually leads him to question his prejudices. Le Guin plays with light and dark as a metaphor for diametrically opposed yet interdependent factors of difference, particularly male/female and peace/war; the result is a powerful disquisition on the male-female dialectic and all its associated assumptions and prejudices. Both philosophical and political in its keen exploration of modes of thought, while still a damn good adventure, Le Guin's tale has a contemporary slant: it stands as a startlingly up-to-date warning to any nation appointing itself a benevolent empire without cultural understanding of other countries. It's a unique strength of her science fiction that such warnings have become increasingly prescient after a generation.

## Read on
*The Dispossessed*; *A Wizard of Earthsea*

Marge Piercy, *Woman on the Edge of Time*; Joanna Russ, *The Female Man*; Sheri S. Tepper, *The Gate to Women's Country*

# JONATHAN LETHEM (b. 1964)

## MOTHERLESS BROOKLYN (1999)

Jonathan Lethem was always going to be cool. Art, writing and activism ran in his family, who lived in a commune at a time when Brooklyn was more edgy than today. An early obsession with music and science fiction translated into his early genre-bending science fiction, but it was his gloriously original hardboiled crime novel *Motherless Brooklyn* that proved his breakthrough book. Orphan Lionel Essrog was taken in fifteen years ago by Frank Minna, now working for him as a gumshoe in a grotty private detective outfit. One night Lionel and his partner lose their boss in a trail case and Frank ends up stabbed to death – an episode with evocative description ▸▸ Raymond Chandler would have been proud of: 'The blood smelled like a thunderstorm coming, like ozone.' The case is on for Lionel and the other three Minna Men to find Frank's murderer and bring him to justice. But Lionel faces one huge obstacle: he has Tourette's. Like ▸▸ Jonathan Safran Foer in *Everything Is Illuminated*, Lethem makes postmodern trickery work for, not against the novel because of his warmth towards the narrator. Humour is very important: Lionel's mind is an entertaining and chaotic place to be. As

Tourettic bombs explode in his brain, Lionel struggles to maintain control of the linguistic shrapnel and physical tics (such as kissing or tapping strangers) to impose order on his disordered mind and the world around it, much as Philip Marlowe tried to correct modern LA through his moral choices. Lionel tells us how the rhyming, scattershot rush of words – a real *tour de force* of writing – 'placate, interpret, massage. Everywhere they're smoothing down imperfections, putting hairs in place, putting ducks in a row, replacing divots'. But Lionel is no Marlowe, whatever he believes, and his mental fragility helps to create a vital *noir* sense of danger. Occasionally Lethem veers too close to pastiche, and the mystery is perhaps less fascinating than Lionel himself, but that is partly testament to the brilliance of the narration. As a bold reinvention of a classic genre, *Motherless Brooklyn* is irresistible.

## 🕮Read on

*Chronic City*; *The Fortress of Solitude*
➤➤ Paul Auster, *The New York Trilogy*; ➤➤ Jonathan Safran Foer, *Everything Is Illuminated*

# JACK LONDON (1876–1916)

## THE CALL OF THE WILD (1903)

Jack London was a prolific writer and his books range from a dystopian novel about the rise of a dictatorship in America (*The Iron Heel*) and a thinly fictionalised account of his own difficulties with alcohol (*John Barleycorn*) to sea stories such as *The Sea-Wolf* and tales of life in prehistoric times (*Before Adam*). However, much his most successful fiction draws on his own experiences as a young man in the Klondike Gold Rush of the 1890s. London wrote many short stories set in the region of Canada where gold was discovered and his most famous novel, *The Call of the Wild*, unfolds against the backdrop of the snowy wilderness of the American North. The story focuses on Buck, a St Bernard dog, who is stolen from his comfortable home in California and taken to the Klondike as a sledge-dog. He passes from owner to owner, each more brutal than the last, until he finds kindness at the hands of John Thornton. But Thornton is killed, Buck's last link with human beings is broken and he escapes to the wild and becomes the leader of a pack of wild dogs. *The Call of the Wild* can be read in many ways. On one level, it is a vividly written, if somewhat bloodthirsty, boy's own adventure story which invites the reader to empathise with Buck in his trials and triumphs. On another the narrative embodies London's ideas about the thin line that divides civilisation from a nature that is very definitely red in tooth and claw. Scratch the surface of society, he says, and you will soon find the brutality and barbarism that lurk beneath. In fact, his prose often suggests a relish for the violence of the beast within. It is London's willingness to acknowledge the power of the primitive and the instinctual that continues to make Buck's story so unforgettable.

**≝Film versions:** *The Call of the Wild* (1935); *The Call of the Wild* (1972)

**≋Read on**
*White Fang* (a companion novel to *The Call of the Wild*); *The Sea-Wolf*
›› Ernest Hemingway, *The Old Man and the Sea*

# NORMAN MAILER (1923–2007)

## THE NAKED AND THE DEAD (1948)

Norman Mailer was a combative figure in American literature for nearly sixty years. In his youth he was an *enfant terrible*. In middle age he was a boozy, brawling polemicist, the scourge of feminists and others who failed to see the world in quite the same way that he did. Even at the very end of his life he was still unafraid to tackle the most ambitious and controversial of themes. His last published novel, *The Castle in the Forest*, took as its subject nothing less than the nature of evil as it blended fact and fiction in a story of the emergence of Adolf Hitler. *The Naked and the Dead* was his first novel, based on his own experiences of serving as a soldier in the South Pacific, and it became a bestseller, propelling Mailer into a fame that he never lost. The book follows the fortunes of a platoon of foot soldiers struggling for possession of the Japanese-held island of Anopopei. (Anopopei is fictional but it resembles many of the small Pacific islands over which the Japanese and the Americans fought so bloodily.) It opens with the invasion of the island and then, in flashbacks, Mailer introduces readers to each of his leading characters, showing how their lives have been shaped by their different experiences of growing up in America and what has brought them to this climactic battle on a distant dot of land in the Pacific. As the action unfolds across seven hundred pages, readers are given a perspective on the entire, bloody progress of the war from the struggles of the poor grunts on the front line to the internal squabbling of the high command. Often overwrought and over-written, peppered with Mailer's slightly ridiculous-sounding, invented expletive (famously he used 'fug' for a then less acceptable four-letter word), *The Naked and the Dead* nonetheless remains the most powerful and ambitious American novel to emerge from the Second World War.

**⬛Film version:** *The Naked and the Dead* (1958)

**📚Read on**
*An American Dream*; *Harlot's Ghost*
James Jones, *From Here to Eternity*; James Salter, *The Hunters*; Robert Stone, *Dog Soldiers*

# BERNARD MALAMUD (1914–86)

## THE ASSISTANT (1957)

Born in Brooklyn, the son of poor Jewish immigrants, Bernard Malamud became one of the leading novelists of the 1950s and 1960s, someone to place alongside ›› Philip Roth and ›› Saul Bellow in any canon of great Jewish-American writers. His first novel, published in 1952, was *The Natural*, the story of an ageing baseball player attempting a comeback many years after his career was derailed when he was shot by a deranged obsessive. Five years later, Malamud published *The Assistant*, a book which engaged more directly with his own childhood experiences and his sense of Jewish-American identity. Morris Bober and his wife Ida run a small grocery store in Brooklyn in the years immediately after the Second World War. Times are hard and they get even harder when the shop is robbed and Morris is beaten up. A man named Frank Alpine arrives in the neighbourhood, down on his luck, and eventually begins to work for Morris as an assistant. It soon becomes apparent to the reader, if not necessarily to the other characters, that Frank is one of the men who robbed the store but his motives in returning to the scene of his crime are unclear. Soon his willingness to work hard shows results. The store begins to do better and Morris comes to enjoy the company of his assistant. However, Frank's growing attraction to the Bobers' daughter, Helen, threatens complications and he has begun to pilfer from the till. When Morris catches him stealing and Helen rejects him after he forces himself upon her, Frank appears to have lost all he had gained in his time as the store's assistant. The rest of the novel charts his attempts to redeem himself both in his own eyes and those of the Bobers. A morality tale of great subtlety and scope, *The Assistant* is arguably the finest achievement of Malamud's career.

**Film version:** *The Assistant* (1997)

**Read on**
*God's Grace*; *The Natural*
>> Saul Bellow, *Herzog*; >> Henry Roth, *Call It Sleep*

## READ ON A THEME: THE JEWISH EXPERIENCE

>> E.L. Doctorow, *World's Fair*
Rebecca Goldstein, *The Mind-Body Problem*
Cynthia Ozick, *The Puttermesser Papers*
Chaim Potok, *The Chosen*
>> Philip Roth, *Portnoy's Complaint*
Isaac Bashevis Singer, *Enemies: A Love Story*

# ARMISTEAD MAUPIN (b. 1944)

## TALES OF THE CITY (1978)

Novelist and journalist Armistead Maupin can justly claim to be one of the people who brought gay culture to a mainstream audience, though he himself was bred in the conservative and Christian environs of North Carolina. After a spell in the navy, including in Vietnam, he carved out a career in reporting, leading to a post with the Associated Press in San Francisco in 1971. It was in that bohemian, cultured city – with its thriving gay scene – that Maupin came out and where *Tales of the City* came into existence, first as a newspaper serial of 1976, then blossoming into a six-volume series. The first of the series – which thanks to its serial nature, is episodically written – *Tales of the City* introduces a cast of characters who slip into and out of each others' lives, much of the action taking place at a boarding house at 28 Barbary Street owned by hippyish Mrs Madrigal. There's the naïve, lonely Cleveland woman Mary Ann Singleton; out and proud unemployed Michael 'Mouse' Tolliver; Mona Ramsey, a coke-sniffing copywriter – and the people they work for, fall in love with, live with, sleep with. Addictive, hip and funny, Maupin hit upon a uniquely San Franciscan sensibility: here the summer of love survived after Vietnam, before the cataclysm of AIDS, and though the time-setting opening conversation is of the Zodiac killer, the tone is gossipy rather than analytical. Here is gay culture's golden age at its exciting epicentre, and Maupin revels in it and the soap opera-like lives of his characters. He embodies San Francisco as much as Ginsberg or ❯❯ Kerouac – and is more likeable than both. There's no doubting Maupin's book is sentimental, idealistic, frothy and dialogue-heavy like contemporary chick lit, but that was to his advantage. Maupin managed to sell mainstream readers on the gay life by not trying to shock or browbeat, but through the warmth of his characterisation, gentle humour, and by contexualising the gay experience. Perhaps it gave some the courage to come out, for many it made gay culture cool, but importantly he showed that love is love whoever is involved. He tore down segregation simply through charm.

### ⮞Read on
*More Tales of the City*; *Sure of You*
>> Truman Capote, *Other Voices, Other Rooms*; Michael Cunningham, *A Home at the End of the World*; Andrew Holleran, *Dancer from the Dance*

# WILLIAM MAXWELL (1908–2000)

## THE CHATEAU (1961)
For nearly forty years William Maxwell was the fiction editor of *The New Yorker* and, in that role, he commissioned work from many of the major American writers of the twentieth century from >> J.D. Salinger and >> John Updike to >> Vladimir Nabokov and Eudora Welty. He was also a highly gifted writer himself. His short stories, published in more than half a dozen volumes from the 1940s to the 1990s, are distinguished by

the elegance and precision of their language. His first novel was published in 1934 and another five appeared over the next fifty years. *They Came Like Swallows* is a novella based on Maxwell's own experiences as a boy in the Midwest during the 1918 flu epidemic; *So Long, See You Tomorrow* is the touching story of an old man remembering a boyhood friendship and the tragedy, only half-understood at the time, which blighted it. However, his finest work may well be *The Chateau* which tells the story of a young, prosperous American couple in France a few years after the end of the Second World War. Harold and Barbara Rhodes have come to stay as paying guests at the Chateau Beaumesnil and they arrive with high hopes of immersing themselves in French culture. Instead they find themselves forced to contemplate 'their isolation as tourists in a country they could look at but never really know'. The owner of the chateau is unimpressed by their attempts to speak her language and resentful of the circumstances which have driven her to the ignominious expedient of opening the doors of her home to strangers. Harold and Barbara are eager to please but, as Maxwell shows in a series of beautifully orchestrated comic set-pieces, their efforts to do so are doomed. Like an updated version of a novel by ❯❯ Henry James, *The Chateau* shows the Old World and the New struggling to communicate across an abyss of linguistic and cultural misunderstanding.

## ❧Read on

*All The Days and Nights* (collected short stories); *So Long, See You Tomorrow*; *They Came Like Swallows*
John Williams, *Stoner*

# CORMAC McCARTHY (b. 1933)

## BLOOD MERIDIAN (1985)

Born in Rhode Island and raised as a Catholic in Tennessee, Cormac McCarthy was the third of six children. He began winning writing prizes while at university; his first novel, *The Orchard Keeper*, was published in 1965. A wide readership eluded him (at least until the appearance of *All The Pretty Horses* in 1992) but he received plenty of critical acclaim, particularly for *Blood Meridian*. In this brutal Western, a Tennessee teenager known as 'the kid' leaves the US frontier for Mexico with a band of soldiers aiming to acquire land for themselves. In a scene of stomach-churning ferocity, most are killed by an Apache war party. The kid survives and falls in with a band of scalphunters, led by real-life figure John Glanton. And so the Americans, 'half crazed with the enormity of their own presence in that immense and bloodslaked waste', begin a grand orgy of slaughter. *Blood Meridian* offers a radical revision of the Western mythos: there are no 'goodies' or 'baddies', just murderers, slain animals, poverty, racism and exploitation. McCarthy provides no safety net, only a stunning subversion of America's founding myths via incredibly extreme violence. In one infernal discovery, a tree hangs with babies' corpses; in another, 'One of the mares had foaled in the desert and this frail form soon hung skewered on a paloverde pole over the raked coals while the Delawares passed among themselves a gourd containing the curdled milk taken from its stomach'. McCarthy's poetic, punctuation-light prose creates hellish visions worthy of Dante and Milton, filtered through the dizzying imagery of ➤➤ Faulkner and his own earlier Southern Gothic. The land itself becomes a dusty, writhing Fury – only McCarthy could write: 'The crumple butcherpaper mountains lay in sharp shadowfold under the long blue dusk ...' More recent novels like *No Country for Old Men* and *The Road* have made McCarthy the darling of film-makers but *Blood Meridian* is the ultimate argument for the immediacy of the written word; without the remove provided by a screen, its relentless horror is overwhelming, an ageless picture of mankind's viciousness. As McCarthy says: 'How these things end. In confusion and curses and blood.'

### ☙Read on
*All the Pretty Horses* (the first volume in McCarthy's 'Border Trilogy'); *No Country for Old Men*; *The Road*
**»** William Faulkner, *Light in August*; Ron Hansen, *Desperadoes*; Jim Thompson, *Pop. 1280*

---

## READONATHEME: THE WEST

Walter Van Tilburg Clark, *The Ox-Bow Incident*
Pete Dexter, *Deadwood*
Thomas Eidson, *St Agnes' Stand*
Zane Grey, *Riders of the Purple Sage*
A.B. Guthrie, *The Big Sky*
Oakley Hall, *Warlock*
Elmore Leonard, *Hombre*
Larry McMurtry, *Lonesome Dove*
Charles Portis, *True Grit*
Jack Schaefer, *Shane*

# JAY McINERNEY (b. 1955)

## BRIGHT LIGHTS, BIG CITY (1984)

'You are not the kind of guy who would be at a place like this at this time of the morning.' So begins McInerney's semi-autobiographical narrative, written (unusually) in the second-person. His unnamed protagonist, a fact checker – as McInerney was himself for *The New Yorker* – has been left by his model wife, Amanda; his mother has also recently died. His life left essentially meaningless, he divines meaning solely from the objects Amanda left in their apartment, and from nights out seeking cocaine and women with his friend Tad. McInerney and his novel defined 1980s New York: self-obsessed, glamorous, ambitious and a place where Manhattan was everything, the 'burbs nothing. This was the era of excess, and no one lived or wrote it better than McInerney and his so-called 'literary brat pack' friends, including ›› Bret Easton Ellis – there's more white powder in McInerney's story than a season at Aspen. Yet in *Bright Lights, Big City*, hedonism is also symptomatic of a city that's lost its meaning to the main character, and New York becomes like a glitterball: glitzy on the outside but – without people to love – hollow. It's because of, and not despite, the drugs that McInerney's tale is unexpectedly moving, evoking a sense of loss and nihilism amid a modern world that's ceased to care. A genuinely experimental author who studied with ›› Raymond Carver – whom he names as one of his favourite writers – it does him an injustice merely to scratch the surface of his work. As a young writer in his mid-twenties, he was the bad-boy writer who'd nailed it first time and, via some very public marriage break-ups and extrovert behaviour, fell in and out of love with the press; it's a legacy McInerney has never truly escaped since. His hugely effective crystalisation of that time in *Bright Lights, Big City* may ensure he never will.

📖**Film version:** *Bright Lights, Big City* (1988, starring Michael J. Fox)

📚**Read on**
*Story of My Life*; *Brightness Falls*
>> Bret Easton Ellis, *The Rules of Attraction*; Tama Janowitz, *Slaves of New York*

## READ ON A THEME: NEW YORK THROUGH THE DECADES

Kevin Baker, *Dreamland*
Caleb Carr, *The Alienist*
>> Don DeLillo, *Great Jones Street*
>> Henry James, *Washington Square*
>> Jonathan Lethem, *The Fortress of Solitude*
Claire Messud, *The Emperor's Children*
Steven Millhauser, *Martin Dressler: The Story of an American Dreamer*
Damon Runyon, *Guys and Dolls*
Hubert Selby Jr, *Last Exit to Brooklyn*
>> Jane Smiley, *Duplicate Keys*

# HERMAN MELVILLE (1819–91)

## MOBY-DICK (1851)

Herman Melville began his career as a bank clerk, but it was his time on a whaling ship in the South Seas that shaped his writing in the 1840s and 1850s. Living as a married man back in New York, and as a neighbour to writer ›› Nathaniel Hawthorne, he produced a genuine masterpiece in *Moby-Dick*, first published in 1851. The book is partially based on real-life stories of whaling disasters, but its ambition is almost limitless. 'Call me Ishmael', says the book's narrator in his famous and memorable first line. Ishmael is an occasional sailor who goes adventuring 'whenever it is a damp, drizzly November in my soul'. En route he befriends regal 'cannibal' harpooner Queequeg, and in Nantucket the pair board the whaling ship *Pequod*. The ship, they discover, is ruled over by the monomaniacal Captain Ahab, a man with one 'barbaric white leg' honed from whale ivory and who gives Ishmael 'foreboding shivers'. Well might Ishmael fear, for Ahab is engaged on an obsessive revenge mission to kill the great white whale Moby-Dick, a quest that will lead him and his crew to destruction. As heady in 'fact' as it is in epic metaphysical sweep, *Moby-Dick* is a startling and gripping allegory in which the whale may represent the devil Leviathan, or fate as proscribed by God, and where either Ahab or the whale or both are symbolically crucified by his obsession. On the one hand *Moby-Dick* is awash with Romanticism: the clash of nature and man, the spiritual tempest, the odyssey of a ruined soul – in this it resembles Shelley's *Frankenstein* or Conrad's *Heart of Darkness*. Yet its style is groundbreaking in its proto-modernism: Melville plays with narrative in entirely unexpected ways, from leaps into the second person to technical treatises on whaling. This disconnect left Melville's masterwork underappreciated during his life, and it was not until the spiritual cataclysm of the First World War and the birth of the Modernist movement that it took its rightful place in American literature.

◀**Film version:** *Moby-Dick* (1956, directed by John Huston and starring Gregory Peck as Captain Ahab)

**Read on**
*Billy Budd*; *Typee*
Andrea Barrett, *The Voyage of the Narwhal*; Richard Henry Dana, *Two Years Before the Mast*; ▶▶ Ernest Hemingway, *The Old Man and the Sea*

# MARGARET MITCHELL (1900–49)

## GONE WITH THE WIND (1936)

A huge bestseller when it first appeared (it still is) and the basis of one of the most famous of all Hollywood movies, *Gone with the Wind* made Margaret Mitchell, who had been working on the novel for the best part of a decade, famous around the world. In the book, the American Civil War is the backdrop for a panoramic lament for the lost glories of the American South and for the story of headstrong beauty Scarlett O'Hara and her turbulent relationship with two men. When the novel opens, just before the outbreak of hostilities, Scarlett is a spoilt teenage belle living on her family plantation, Tara, in Georgia. She is infatuated with the handsome son of a neighbouring plantation owner, Ashley Wilkes, but he marries another woman. The war then changes everything. The man Scarlett married on the rebound from Ashley is killed. Her life becomes a struggle to survive and to retain and rebuild Tara which is destroyed by the Yankee army. To achieve this goal she is prepared to do almost anything. At the end of the war Scarlett renews her relationship with Rhett Butler, a caddish charmer whom she first met in the pre-war years. She eventually marries him but happiness still eludes her. Few historical novels have the sweeping power, the sense of ordinary lives caught up in great events, that *Gone with the Wind* possesses but it was destined to be the only fiction that Margaret Mitchell published. Thirteen years after her *magnum opus* appeared, she was knocked down by a speeding car in an Atlanta street and died five days later without regaining consciousness. In the sixty years since her death *Gone with the Wind*, her solitary triumph, has retained its status as one of the best loved and best known of all American novels.

◀**Film version:** *Gone with the Wind* (1939, starring Vivien Leigh as Scarlett O'Hara, Clark Gable as Rhett Butler and Leslie Howard as Ashley Wilkes)

**☙Read on**
Alexandra Ripley, *Scarlett* (a sequel to Mitchell's book written some fifty years later)
Hervey Allen, *Anthony Adverse* (another bestselling historical epic by an American writer of the 1930s); Ross Lockridge Jr, *Raintree County*;

Margaret Walker, *Jubilee* (the story of a female slave in Georgia before, during and after the Civil War)

# TONI MORRISON (b. 1931)

## BELOVED (1987)

Toni Morrison's work, especially the Pulitzer Prize-winning *Beloved*, has transformed debates about race and gender in the later twentieth century. From a working-class Ohio background, Morrison has gone on to match high-flying academic and literary achievement with a public consciousness that makes her one of the most significant African-American voices. *Beloved*'s uncompromising story, based on the real life of Margaret Garner, begins as former slave Sethe and her eighteen-year-old-daughter Denver are reunited with Paul D, a fellow former slave from a Kentucky plantation ironically called Sweet Home. Their home is haunted and the family ostracised by the local community, a legacy from events at Sweet Home. There Sethe was subjected to vicious, dehumanising sexual and physical abuse so bad that, when the owner found them after an escape, she slit her two-year-old daughter's throat rather than see her recaptured. Meanwhile, in the present, a mysterious young woman named 'Beloved' arrives to live with Sethe ... Morrison uses folkloric and supernatural elements to elevate the impact of the very real horrors suffered by Sethe and her family, conveyed in Faulknerian prose replete with Biblical power. *Beloved* is one of the most striking modern examples of the novel as social document, in the manner of Tolstoy or Primo Levi; history in the book is an omnipresent witness to the crimes perpetuated on Sethe, specifically, and on black Africans generally, the arrival of the ghostly Beloved and the book's non-linear narrative keeping Sethe's current existence tethered to her past; Morrison also dedicates the book to 'Sixty Million and more', in reference to the African multitudes who died being shipped to America. Where ❯❯ Harper Lee charms, Morrison attacks: the love that Sethe carries – and then subdues to protect her vulnerability – is visceral, ferocious, and the only thing stronger than the violence of the white system. Above all, the book is about freedom – even the freedom to kill out of love. By raising the ghosts of slavery, *Beloved* highlights an unreconciled bloody past that the USA must face unblinkingly, or else give in to the tacit racism that still hides in America's endless vistas.

**⛶Film version:** *Beloved* (1998, starring Oprah Winfrey as Sethe)

**⮧Read on**
*A Mercy*; *Paradise*; *Song of Solomon*
Edward P. Jones, *The Known World*; ❯❯ Alice Walker, *Meridian*

## READONATHEME: UP FROM SLAVERY
(African-American fiction)

Octavia Butler, *Kindred*
Ernest J. Gaines, *The Autobiography of Miss Jane Pittman*
Chester Himes, *If He Hollers Let Him Go*
Charles Johnson, *Middle Passage*
Gayl Jones, *Corregidora*
Nella Larsen, *Passing*
Ann Petry, *The Street*
Ishmael Reed, *Mumbo Jumbo*

# WALTER MOSLEY (b. 1952)

## DEVIL IN A BLUE DRESS (1990)

In the course of a prolific career, Walter Mosley has written fiction that has ranged from *RL's Dream*, the story of an old blues guitarist reminiscing about his meeting with Robert Johnson, king of the Delta blues singers, and a man notorious for having sold his soul to the Devil in return for unrivalled musical talent and fame, to a series of novels featuring Socrates Fortlow, a tough and wise ex-con, trying to go straight and finding it a difficult task. However, his best-known work and his finest achievement remains the sequence of novels focusing on the life of Ezekiel ('Easy') Rawlins, a black Second World War veteran who sets ups as a private eye in Los Angeles. The novels follow his fortunes from the late 1940s to the 1960s and the first is *Devil in a Blue Dress*. A racial inversion of ⟩⟩ Raymond Chandler's classic *noir* novel *Farewell, My Lovely*, Mosley's tale begins when Easy loses his job at an airplane factory and, anxious that he might lose his home as well, is desperate to earn money. Through a friend he meets a man named DeWitt Albright who hires him to find a missing white woman. As he searches for Daphne Monet, a rich man's mistress with a fondness for black jazz clubs and jazz players, Rawlins enters new realms of racial tension and violence, finding himself forced to straddle two worlds in order to survive. Murders occur for which he becomes a suspect. Albright turns out to have secrets that he has been unwilling to confide. Easy's psychopathic friend, 'Mouse', turns up at an opportune moment to become his unpredictable assistant in the search for the truth. In *Devil in a Blue Dress* and the series of books which have followed it, Mosley provides a brilliant update on Chandler's mean streets, viewed from a black perspective.

◣**Film version:** *Devil in a Blue Dress* (1995, starring Denzel Washington as Easy Rawlins)

≋**Read on**
*A Red Death* (the next in the Rawlins series); *Always Outnumbered, Always Outgunned* (the first Socrates Fortlow book)
⟩⟩ Raymond Chandler, *Farewell, My Lovely*; Chester Himes, *A Rage in Harlem*

# VLADIMIR NABOKOV (1899–1977)

## LOLITA (1955)

Born in St Petersburg into a wealthy and prominent family of lawyers and politicians, Nabokov was one of the millions of Russians whose lives were turned upside down by the October Revolution of 1917. He went into exile in the West, first studying in Cambridge and then living in Berlin (where his father was assassinated by a political opponent) and gradually becoming a well-known novelist and poet in the Russian émigré community there. Nabokov wrote in his native language until 1940, when he crossed the Atlantic and settled in the USA; thereafter, he worked in English, and also translated and revised his earlier works. He became a naturalised American citizen in 1945. Few novels have proved as controversial as *Lolita* which was turned down by several American publishers before it was published in Paris by the Olympia Press. When it did eventually appear in an American edition, it was hailed by some as a work of genius, by others as erudite pornography. The novel is the story of Humbert Humbert, a scholarly adorer of what he calls 'nymphets', those girls between the ages of nine and fourteen who possess a particular allure for him. It focuses on his obsessive love/lust for Dolores Haze, also known as Lolita, the just-pubescent daughter of his landlady in a small New England town. Told in Humbert's own voice, characterised by flamboyant wordplay and elaborate parades of his bookish learning, it records his marriage to Lolita's mother, his plot to become the nymphet's sole guardian, his seduction of her, their helter-skelter journey across America and his eventual loss of the love of his life. Disturbing in its subject matter,

*Lolita* is a work of brilliantly perverse and comic artistry in which Nabokov leads readers further and further into a narrative that is never quite what it seems.

◀**Film version:** *Lolita* (1962, directed by Stanley Kubrick and starring James Mason as Humbert Humbert); *Lolita* (1997, directed by Adrian Lyne and starring Jeremy Irons as Humbert Humbert)

**≋Read on**
*The Gift* (first written in Russian in the 1930s and translated into English under Nabokov's supervision in the 1960s); *Pale Fire*; *Pnin*
John Barth, *Giles Goat-Boy*; Donald Barthelme, *Snow White*

# JOYCE CAROL OATES (b. 1938)

## BLONDE (2000)
Joyce Carol Oates grew up in the countryside around Lockport, New York, in a happy working-class home. Following university, she married and moved to Detroit, a city whose turmoil informed her superb 1969 novel *them*. In the decades since the publication of her first book, a collection of short stories, in 1963, she has been one of America's most prolific and versatile authors. Fact and fiction frequently meet in her many tough, compelling reflections on modern America, and they do so

in *Blonde*. Who is more iconically American than the novel's central character, Marilyn Monroe? A 'radically distilled life in the form of fiction', as Oates describes it, *Blonde* takes the legendary bombshell from a humble, tough childhood as Norma Jeane Baker, living with her mentally ill mother Gladys, to fame and fortune as Marilyn. The thread that runs throughout the book is the young woman's need to be loved and the exploitation that follows from it. Like ›› Nathanael West, Oates is merciless about Hollywood's palsied soul. Norma Jeane's whole existence is staked out from the start like a film role. As Oates says, 'Always there is a script'. The Hollywood machine, with its domineering men, decides her fate. The advice Gladys gives to her – 'Remember, Norma Jeane – die at the right time' – reminds us that as a celebrity commodity, early death just aids the sell. Switching between the first and third person, and using pseudonyms for real figures – Joe DiMaggio is the Ex-Athlete, Arthur Miller the Playwright, John F. Kennedy the President – Oates' obfuscations incriminate us by our need for tittle-tattle – we want the dirt, we want the names. Conversely, Norma Jeane herself is lost to us, unknowable – we only see Monroe, that goddess-like body we owned through the media, but without the troublesome reality of genuine physicality. This hypocrisy is made explicit by Oates' portrayal of the famous dress-billowing scene above a subway vent in *The Seven Year Itch*: 'Without the dress the girl would be female meal, raw and exposed'. *Blonde* is horribly affecting, reminding us of the precious, damaged soul rattling around inside that famous body, its voice once full of verve and love for the movies. Like her British counterpart in fairytale tragedy, Princess Diana, here is the physical undoing of a 'Fair Princess' in which we are all accountable.

≈**Read on**
*The Falls*; *them*
Joan Didion, *Play It as It Lays*; >> Norman Mailer, *Of Women and Their Elegance*

# FLANNERY O'CONNOR (1925–64)

## WISE BLOOD (1952)

Soon after the publication of Flannery O'Connor's first novel, *Wise Blood*, in 1952, one of her elderly aunts was heard saying to a neighbour, 'I don't know where Flannery met those people she wrote about, but it was certainly not in *my* house'. Her aunt's puzzlement seems understandable. Where exactly did they come from, the Deep South grotesques, religious obsessives and violent outsiders who parade through the stories of Flannery O'Connor? To many of those who knew her, little about her suggested possession of such an unsettling imagination. Shy, unmarried and devoutly Catholic, she spent most of her days living with her mother on a family farm near the Georgia town of Milledgeville and died before she was forty from the ravages of the autoimmune disease lupus. Many critics would argue that O'Connor's finest work can be found in her short stories and there is no doubt that some of these are amongst the most memorable and compelling examples of the form published in America in the twentieth century.

However, the two novels that appeared in her lifetime are equally original. *Wise Blood* follows the fortunes of its central character, Hazel Motes, a confused young man who travels to a Tennessee town after years in the Army. Hazel yearns for spiritual truths but has turned against religion and is now moved to start advocating his own gospel of the 'Church without Christ'. He meets with a whole gallery of grotesques in his new role, including a deceitful preacher named Asa Hawks, who claims falsely to have blinded himself in the service of the Lord, Hawks's sexy daughter Sabbath Lily, a disturbed teenager called Enoch Emery and an evangelist known as Onnie Jay Holy who appropriates Hazel's ideas for his own purposes. One of the most consistently surprising works of what has been called 'Southern Gothic', *Wise Blood* is a book that mingles black farce with religious debate and allegory to create a work of fiction like few others in the history of American literature.

**Film version:** *Wise Blood* (1979, directed by John Huston and starring Brad Dourif as Hazel Motes)

**Read on**

*The Violent Bear It Away* (O'Connor's only other novel); *A Good Man Is Hard to Find*; *Everything That Rises Must Converge* (two volumes of short stories)

Davis Grubb, *The Night of the Hunter*; Carson McCullers, *The Heart Is a Lonely Hunter*; Eudora Welty, *The Optimist's Daughter*

**READ**ON**A**THEME: DEEP SOUTH

Hamilton Basso, *The View from Pompey's Head*
Pete Dexter, *Paris Trout*
James Dickey, *Deliverance*
>> William Faulkner, *Absalom! Absalom!*
Tim Gautreaux, *The Clearing*
Shirley Ann Grau, *The Keepers of the House*
Allan Gurganus, *Oldest Confederate Widow Tells All*
Peter Taylor, *A Summons to Memphis*
Robert Penn Warren, *All the King's Men*
Thomas Wolfe, *Look Homeward, Angel*

# CHUCK PALAHNIUK (b. 1962)

## FIGHT CLUB (1996)

Hailing from Washington State and educated as a journalist in Oregon, Chuck Palahniuk has long been fascinated with subcultures and life outside the mainstream. For a time he worked with the homeless and the terminally ill, and has been a member of the mischief-creating Cacophony Society, the apparent inspiration for Project Mayhem in his 1996 debut novel (and the basis for a hit, faithful film adaptation), *Fight Club*. It begins as it ends, with a gun in the mouth. Elliptically told in minimal, >> Raymond Carver-style prose, *Fight Club* is a perfectly conceived metaphysical thriller. The novel's unnamed protagonist suffers from chronic insomnia and premillennial *ennui*, attending self-help groups for the terminally ill just to feel alive, where he meets another death-tourist, Marla Singer. He falls under the spell of Tyler Durden, a charismatic, philosophising ultra-male, and together they establish fight club, an illegal bare-knuckle outlet for men to rediscover their primal masculinity – provided 'you don't talk about fight club'. Tyler begins an affair with Marla and his monomania transforms fight club's blue-collar heroes into the sinister secret army Project Mayhem. Meanwhile, sleeplessness robs the protagonist of the last vestiges of reality ... Palahniuk's gripping, propulsive story fashions the holy trinity of *fin de siècle* thought – Nietzsche, Marx and Freud – into an attack on the injuries post-war American society has inflicted on men. He finds a rich seam of dark humour in the absurdities of modern life, from identikit Ikea furniture to the euphemistic language of self-help groups and health ads. In one stomach-churning satirical gag, collagen removed by liposuction from the rich is fashioned by Tyler into soap to be sold back to them at vast expense. Like other great transgressive authors from ›› William S. Burroughs to ›› Bret Easton Ellis, Palahniuk makes serious points via shock and awe – the shadow memories of David Koresh, the Manson family and Timothy McVeigh lurk in Tyler's cult. But it's also a beautifully fashioned apostolic novel filtered through an imagination scraped from the darkest depths of the American psyche. It's a cry from the streets, a fist in the face. Just don't talk about it.

◄**Film version:** *Fight Club* (1999, directed by David Fincher and starring Brad Pitt and Edward Norton)

**≋Read on**
*Choke*; *Haunted*; *Invisible Monsters*
**»** Bret Easton Ellis, *Lunar Park*; Amy Hempel, *The Collected Stories*

# WALKER PERCY (1916–90)

## THE MOVIEGOER (1962)

European existentialist philosophy and the Southern literary tradition come together to create strange and compelling fiction in the work of Walker Percy. Percy was born in Birmingham, Alabama into a distinguished Southern family which included Civil War soldiers, politicians and a number of writers in the ranks of its past and present members. Orphaned as a teenager, when both his parents died within the space of two years (both probably as the result of suicide), he and his brothers were then adopted by a distant cousin, a lawyer and poet who knew many of the leading Southern writers of the day including John Crowe Ransom and Robert Penn Warren. Percy trained as a doctor and may well have followed that career path had he not contracted tuberculosis and been forced to spend long periods in a sanatorium. Instead he became a convert to Catholicism and decided to write. His first novel was not published until he was in his mid-forties. *The Moviegoer* is the story of John 'Binx' Bolling, an investment broker in New Orleans who yearns for greater meaning in his life. Like his creator, Binx is scarred by the suicide of his father when he was younger and adopts a pose of detached *ennui* when confronted by the world. His favourite pastime is going to the movies and the truth is that he prefers the vicarious experiences of the cinema and literature to more direct engagement with others. All this changes as, on the eve of his thirtieth birthday, he embarks on a search for the authenticity he has not previously felt. 'The search,' Binx tells himself, 'is what anyone would undertake if he were not sunk in the everydayness of his own life' and, through it, he gains a glimpse of what redemption from his existential angst might be. Strange and memorable, *The Moviegoer* is the work of a highly original novelist.

🕮**Read on**
*The Last Gentleman*; *The Second Coming*
>> Don DeLillo, *Mao II*; >> John Kennedy Toole, *A Confederacy of Dunces*

# SYLVIA PLATH (1932–63)

## THE BELL JAR (1963)
Sylvia Plath is known for four things: her massively influential poetry; her (short) marriage to poet Ted Hughes; her single, semi-autobiographical novel *The Bell Jar*; and her suicide in London in 1963 at the age of thirty. *The Bell Jar* spells out a version of her life. In it, boyish, bright would-be writer and poet Esther Greenwood spends a

summer between college terms in New York, working with a set of other young women on *Ladies' Day* magazine. In a whirl of glamorous events, men and innumerable career choices, depression (her 'bell jar') encloses Esther and, as she reminisces about her teenage years, her future begins to look very bleak ... What Plath uniquely captures is a one-off point in time in which post-war women seemed to be offered the world, yet remained caged by the social expectations of their parents and men, and in which depression could be a death sentence. Plath's writing hasn't aged one iota. Written without tricks or artifice, it's surprisingly simple for a poet's novel, an initially breezy tone giving way to the doomy, psychologically troubled cynicism of her later poetry. Esther, Plath's apparent alter ego, is both a clever, appealing narrator and somewhat frustrating. She looks down on the overweight or the stupid, but feels increasingly inferior to more successful or prettier people (especially women), praising their 'intuition' – here begins modern status anxiety and body-consciousness, as Esther bemoans, 'I had been inadequate all along, I simply hadn't thought about it.' Esther knows she has a bevy of possibilities ahead of her, but becomes paralysed by indecision so that, like Plath herself, she sees death as the only escape. In a bittersweet denouement, following intensive therapy, Plath allows Esther the happy ending she denied herself. With depression now an accepted illness, something Plath herself aided with this novel, her suicide is also our tragedy, for who knows what this incisive writer might have achieved in years to come.

## ⮃Read on

*Johnny Panic and Bible of Dreams* (short stories and other prose pieces)

Susanna Kaysen, *Girl, Interrupted* (memoir); **››** Ken Kesey, *One Flew Over the Cuckoo's Nest*; Elizabeth Wurtzel, *Prozac Nation*

# EDGAR ALLAN POE (1809–49)

## TALES OF MYSTERY AND IMAGINATION

Edgar Allan Poe's stories, the best of which appeared in a variety of newspapers and magazines in the early 1840s, are brilliantly written, poetic and inescapably bleak and morbid. They are peopled by unfortunates hailing from families beset by decay and incest, and individuals whose minds have wandered or collapsed. Invariably, they dwell on such dark topics as torture, necrophilia and murder and reflect Poe's own obsessions with madness, premature burial and the deaths of beautiful young women. Often they delve into a past that is as much the creation of Poe's perfervid imagination as it is historical reality or travel the world relying on invention as much as fact. In 'The Pit and the Pendulum' an unnamed victim of the Spanish Inquisition faces a series of fiendishly inventive tortures. 'The Premature Burial' is a tale told by a cataleptic who recounts his obsession with the idea that he will be buried alive. In 'The Fall of the House of Usher' the narrator is the helpless witness of the mental disintegration of his hypersensitive friend Roderick Usher and of the terrible fate of his sister Margaret. Poe was also an early exponent of what would now be called genre fiction. In three short stories ('The Murders in the Rue Morgue', 'The Mystery of

Marie Roget' and 'The Purloined Letter'), for example, in which his character, the brilliantly analytical Parisian Auguste Dupin, solves apparently insoluble mysteries, he became one of the founding fathers of detective fiction. Various collections of the short stories have appeared under many different titles since *Tales of the Grotesque and Arabesque* was published in 1840 during Poe's lifetime but *Tales of Mystery and Imagination*, first used as a title in 1908, is the most familiar. Under whatever collective name they appear, the best of Poe's stories are unforgettable and their influence has been felt by countless other writers in the years since his death.

### ⮒Read on

*The Narrative of Arthur Gordon Pym of Nantucket* (Poe's only novel is a strange tale of a sea voyage towards the South Pole)
Charles Brockden Brown, *Wieland* (a novel by one of Poe's predecessors as a writer of Gothic fiction); H.P. Lovecraft, *At the Mountains of Madness and Other Tales of Terror*; ➤ Herman Melville, *Bartleby the Scrivener*

# DAWN POWELL (1896–1965)

## A TIME TO BE BORN (1942)

'For decades,' ›› Gore Vidal once wrote, 'Dawn Powell was always just on the verge of ceasing to be a cult and becoming a major religion.' Now, at last, as her fiction is included in the prestigious Library of America and more and more critics acknowledge her importance, her status as one of the finest American novelists of her time can be confirmed. Extravagant claims have been made for Powell – that she is 'wittier than Dorothy Parker' and 'dissects the rich better than ›› F. Scott Fitzgerald' – and anyone who has not read her fiction might be inclined to take them with a pinch of salt. For anyone who has read *Angels on Toast*, a comedy of bad manners that satirises the vulgarity of 1930s New York businessmen on the make, or *Turn, Magic Wheel*, a story of bitchery and backbiting amongst the literati of the same era, the claims will seem more credible. However, Powell's masterwork is probably *A Time to Be Born*, set in New York in the months before America's entry into the Second World War. 'This was no time to cry over one broken heart,' the novel begins. With war looming, it's a time when moral seriousness should be the order of the day but Powell's characters just can't quite seem to manage to attain it. Amanda Keeler is a self-obsessed novelist with a rich newspaper baron of a husband who is intent on renewing an affair with an old beau named Kenneth Saunders. Vicky Haven, a friend from the boondocks past that Amanda prefers to forget, arrives in New York just in time to be used as a front for her fling with Kenneth but she doesn't count on Vicky and Kenneth falling for one another. Amanda's carefully constructed world begins to unravel.

Funny, perceptive and unsparing in the light it shines on its characters' many failings, *A Time to Be Born* shows just why Powell's admirers think so highly of her.

### ☙Read on

*Angels on Toast*; *The Locusts Have No King*; *Turn, Magic Wheel*
≫ F. Scott Fitzgerald, *The Beautiful and Damned*; Dorothy Parker, *Complete Stories*; ≫ Nathanael West, *Miss Lonelyhearts*


# ANNIE PROULX (b. 1935)

## ACCORDION CRIMES (1996)

Exploration of immigrant identity is a keystone of the Great American Novel. Annie Proulx's consistently harrowing, emotionally exhausting 1996 novel *Accordion Crimes* tackles this with a rare originality and honesty. On publication it shocked those who loved her earlier Pulitzer Prize-winning look at small-town Newfoundland, *The Shipping News*, but in its ambition, breadth and ferocity the later book shows the Wyoming author burrowing still deeper into the social and personal disturbances of American communities. The central immigrant of *Accordion Crimes* is not, however, a person, but the titular instrument, which links the stories of the many lives its touches over the course of a century, starting with its Sicilian maker, who brings it to America but is killed in an anti-Italian riot in 1890. The ethnic groups (among them Polish, Irish, German and Hispanic) into which it passes tremble with possibility, but the vicissitudes of life in their adopted home end in individual cataclysms and bloody accidents. A former journalist and trained historian, Proulx channels her sharp observation and research skills into tumbling, detailed idiomatic prose. The result is dizzying, the whole grotesque cruelty of a life sometimes contained within a single sentence. As with the cowboys in 'Brokeback Mountain' or the fishing community of *The Shipping News*, Proulx shows a ruminative interest in humans' coexistence with nature and with invisible, disappearing working-class existences. Here men live and die by nature's hand, as well as by their own means of industrial or agricultural production, punctuating the book with brutal endings to unassimilated cultures. *Accordion Crimes* exudes a doomy worldview in which the one bright light is the accordion itself, whose music adjusts to the folk art and ethnicity of the player. Its endurance argues for adaptability in modern America, rather than for continuing the divisions experienced and propagated by the ethnic minorities for whom 'Americans' are always the Other. Proulx, a profoundly serious and intelligent author, presents the powerless struggles of meaningless lives as the very fabric of the patchwork American nation. There is no one narrative of America – just the differences in the music of its people.

## ⮨Read on

*The Shipping News*
>> T.C. Boyle, *The Tortilla Curtain*; Elizabeth McCracken, *The Giant's House*; Joy Williams, *The Quick and the Dead*

# THOMAS PYNCHON (b. 1937)

## MASON & DIXON (1997)

Thomas Pynchon made his name with wild, satirical journeys through the 1960s such as *The Crying of Lot 49* which begins with a character named Oedipa Maas setting out to discover why she has been left a legacy by an ex-lover but quickly develops into a crazy tour of counter-cultural California, an exploration of drugs, bizarre sex, psychic sensitivity and absurd politics, centring on a group of oddball characters united in a secret society that is determined to subvert the US postal system. *Gravity's Rainbow* was first published in 1973. This vast ragbag of paranoid fiction and mad erudition, set in a top-secret British centre for covert operations during the Second World War, may well still be Pynchon's masterpiece but it is not a novel for the faint-hearted to tackle. As an introduction to his unique vision of the world, *Mason & Dixon* provides less of a belly-flopping dive into the deep end. A bizarre conflation of history and anachronism, loosely based on the two eighteenth-century surveyors who gave their names to the Mason-Dixon line that divided the North from the South in the American colonies, this is a historical novel like few others. It follows the partnership of the two men, locked together like a showbiz double act, one depressive and gloomy, the other noisy and flamboyant, as they experience both the rational and irrational in the Age of Reason. Set in England, the Cape of Good Hope and pre-Revolutionary America and featuring a cast of characters that ranges from Benjamin Franklin and Dr Johnson to a Chinese feng shui master, *Mason & Dixon* is a book about drawing boundaries that refuses to acknowledge any boundaries itself. History, according to a character in the novel, 'Is too innocent to be left within the reach of anyone in power ... She needs rather to be tended lovingly and honorably by fabulists and counterfeiters ...' There are no finer fabulists and counterfeiters available to tend her in modern American literature than Thomas Pynchon.

### ⮒Read on
*Gravity's Rainbow*; *Vineland*
John Barth, *The Sot-Weed Factor*; William Gaddis, *JR*; Neal Stephenson, *Cryptonomicon*

# MARILYNNE ROBINSON (b. 1943)

## GILEAD (2004)
Marilynne Robinson published her first novel in 1980. *Housekeeping* was the story of two sisters and their eccentric upbringing in a small Midwestern town. Critics were enthralled by the carefully constructed cadences of its poetic prose and by its reworking of familiar motifs in American literature to tell an exclusively female coming-of-age story. *Housekeeping* attracted many awards and much acclaim but, for more than twenty years after its appearance, Robinson published no further novels. She finally broke her silence in 2004 with *Gilead* and readers were able once again to appreciate the beauty of her style and the

subtlety of her intelligence. In this Pulitzer Prize-winning novel, Robinson's narrator is the elderly preacher John Ames. The book takes the shape of a letter Ames, in his seventies in the 1950s, is writing for his young son to read when he grows up. For many decades the old man has been pastor in the small Iowa town that gives the book its title and for most of these years he has been alone. Yet, in his declining years, he has loved and married a much younger woman who has given him a son. For this son, six years old at the time Ames is writing, he wants to provide a summation of his life's work and its meaning, and to set his own life in the longer perspective of those of his father and grandfather. As he writes, Ames is also obliged to face up to new challenges and dilemmas by the return of his godson, the scapegrace Jack Boughton, to Gilead. Robinson has since written a third novel, *Home*, which uses the same characters and some of the same events that she used in *Gilead* but shifts viewpoints and allows readers to experience them through the eyes of Jack Boughton and his sister, Glory. In the three works of fiction she has written in three decades, she has not only proved herself one of the great prose stylists of contemporary American literature but one of its most profound and insightful novelists.

## ᗜRead on
*Home*; *Housekeeping*
>> Wallace Stegner, *Crossing to Safety*

# HENRY ROTH (1906–95)

## CALL IT SLEEP (1934)

Published at the height of the Great Depression in 1934, Henry Roth's modernist novel *Call It Sleep* is one of the definitive accounts of the New York immigrant experience. Roth was just twenty eight when the book was published, but it only found its readership in the 1960s; the author didn't produce another book until his seventies. The book, based on the world of Roth's childhood, opens as Austrian-Jewish immigrants Genya and her tiny son David arrive in a throng of nationalities at New York's Ellis Island in 1907, met by the family's father, short-tempered, bitter working-man Albert Schearl. In the years to come, Albert, who remains a stranger in a strange land, terrorises his family, shutting them in the cellar. David clings to his devoted mother, who can only speak Yiddish. Into this tinderbox Roth drops a series of firecrackers, as the artistic, sensitive young David begins to open up to the Lower East Side slums around him. *Call It Sleep* is a masterpiece of linguistic athletics. Roth uses the contrast between the Biblical tones of Yiddish spoken within the family with the coarse, phonetically written Gentile dialogue to drive a wall between the Schearls and the New Yorkers inhabiting the local tenements – they are very much old country aliens whose arrival in the 'Golden Land', as Genya describes it, is more blessing than curse. As David escapes his father's tyranny, his Jewish identity and almost Oedipal love for his mother are challenged by his admiration for the independence and freedom of Catholic boy Leo, the trauma of first sexual encounters and his desire for a rosary. Alongside Roth's verbal innovation, his triumphs are the Dickensian characterisation and elegant sensual descriptions that texture the novel – despite its realistic setting, David's intensely interior tale owes much to Joyce and *Ulysses*. David is like a crab with a fractured shell, and each slam of the hammer – from his father, from slum life – threatens to shatter his carapace. His story is full of pain but, like the immigrant experience itself, promises an electric bolt of hope at the end.

⇌**Read on**

*Mercy of a Rude Stream* (Roth's four-volume return to fiction after a fifty-year absence)

›› Saul Bellow, *Herzog*; Harold Brodkey, *The Runaway Soul*; Abraham Cahan, *The Rise of David Levinsky* (first published in 1917, this is an autobiographical novel about a Jewish immigrant in New York from an earlier generation)

# PHILIP ROTH (b. 1933)

## AMERICAN PASTORAL (1997)

Philip Roth was born in 1933 in Newark, New Jersey to first-generation Jewish-American parents, a background that informs the self-reflexive fiction that arguably makes him America's greatest living novelist. As the natural successor to ›› Saul Bellow, who taught him at the University of Chicago, Roth writes stories of Jewish-American identity, familial strife and sexual negotiations which trace the pathology of change in America. The Pulitzer Prize-winning *American Pastoral* (1997) is an archetypal example of his mature later novels. The book is inspired by his Newark upbringing and told in the dry, confessional tones of Roth's 'alter-brain', writer Nathan Zuckerman, as he discovers what became of one-time school sports champ Seymour 'Swede' Levov since his heyday in the 1940s. At first, the Swede lives the American Dream, marrying beautiful 'shiksa' and former Miss New Jersey, Dawn Dwyer; fulfilling generational ideals by making his father's leather glove-making business a success, and moving to bourgeois hamlet Old Rimrock with Dawn and their daughter Merry. But by the 1960s social disorder and the Vietnam War divide the family as Merry embraces militant anti-establishment thinking and the Swede's moral surety speeds the family's implosion. While Zuckerman and his human subject yearn for a lost collective past, in reality the Swede's life and the American Dream burned in the social conflagration of the 1960s: the factory workers face race riots and creeping urban blight; light of the Swede's life Merry commits a terrorist atrocity in the name of freedom; perfect Dawn confesses to infidelity. To Zuckerman, the Swede's 'Aryan' good looks and physical talent embodied post-war America in its shiny golden prime; his Job-like suffering mirrors the nation's crumbling utopianism. And, cleverly, Roth puts subjectivity into play, as Zuckerman jigsaws together his assumptions with the tragic truth, filling in the blanks with imagined episodes. In *American Pastoral*, what you are and what you want to be destroys you. If Roth is literature's Bob Dylan – a simultaneously revealing and self-obscuring storyteller with an incredible hit-rate of classics – then *American Pastoral* is his *Highway*

*61 Revisited*, a furious, tender and sly document of faith's dismantlement and a subsequent emotional dislocation that will resonate for decades to come.

## ⮑Read on
*Portnoy's Complaint*; *Sabbath's Theater*
>> Saul Bellow, *Herzog*; >> Bernard Malamud, *Dubin's Lives*

# J.D. SALINGER (1919–2010)

## THE CATCHER IN THE RYE (1951)
Legendarily reclusive author J.D. Salinger may have written only one novel, but what a novel it is. After years of gestation, *The Catcher in the Rye* emerged in 1951, rolling hero Holden Caulfield's story into the author's own experience of being a flighty youth sent to, and then expelled from, an expensive private school. Like a modern Huckleberry Finn, rebellious sixteen-year-old Holden is half tearaway, half wise man. After the expulsion, he runs off to New York until his well-to-do parents cool off. But for all the feelings of freedom and spontaneity he relishes, Holden carries with him an extreme sadness: the death of his younger brother Allie. Holden is a charismatic and unreliable narrator – 'I'm the most terrific liar you ever saw in your life', he tells us – and his direct and splendidly idiosyncratic language conveys what at first seems to be

a to-hell-with-it-all attitude. The archetypal teenager, he despises 'phonies', loves women but can't relate to them, and wants to experience everything the big city has to offer. Yet for all the urban whirl, he never quite connects with New York life: despite his efforts to drink with cabbies or bed attractive girls, Holden remains an observer, looking on with anger, empathy, excitement or simply boredom. For all his cynical adolescent shell, Holden cares deeply: for his almost-girl-friend Jane, for people worse off than him, and most of all for his dead brother Allie and the family life lost with Allie's passing. In one heartbreaking scene, a lonely Holden hangs around a museum with a present for his kid sister Phoebe on the chance she shows up. Salinger evokes the backyard ritual of a ball tossed around between siblings in Allie's poem-scrawled baseball mitt, thus contrasting the individualist urban modernity of New York – with its exploitation and degradation – with a collective past of mutual support. His hero's rebelliousness, which teenagers respond to and Salinger's enemies object to, is a smokescreen. Holden Caulfield is a thoroughly believable human being adrift in the modern world and in need of comfort – that's something we can all relate to.

## ⮒Read on

*Franny and Zooey*; *Raise High the Roofbeam, Carpenters* (two collections of novellas about the Glass family)
S.E. Hinton, *The Outsiders*; John Knowles, *A Separate Peace*; ▶▶ Mark Twain, *The Adventures of Huckleberry Finn*

# JANE SMILEY (b. 1949)

## A THOUSAND ACRES (1991)

Jane Smiley has published just over a dozen novels in the decades since her 1980 debut with *Barn Blind*. These have ranged from an epic historical novel set in the battleground between pro- and anti-slave factions that was Kansas in the 1850s (*The All-True Travels and Adventures of Lydie Newton*) via an ambitious saga set in a Norse settlement in medieval Greenland (*The Greenlanders*) to a contemporary Decameron in which a Hollywood writer and his guests swap gossip and stories as they engage in ever more complicated emotional and sexual entanglements (*Ten Days in the Hills*). *A Thousand Acres*, which won Smiley the Pulitzer Prize for Fiction in 1992, is a story set in the American Midwest that echoes the events described in Shakespeare's *King Lear*. In Smiley's novel, the Lear-like character is a farmer and the inheritance he bestows on his daughters is not a kingdom but a farm in Iowa. Larry Cook is growing old and he decides to make arrangements for his farm to pass into the joint ownership of Ginny, Rose and Caroline, his children. The youngest of his daughters, Caroline, who has moved away from the family to become a lawyer, refuses to accept her share of the farm and her action in doing so precipitates events which lead to the revelation of long-suppressed family secrets. The novel is narrated by Ginny (the Goneril figure) who records her father's rapid descent into violent and abusive madness. To the outside world, this madness seems a consequence of the heartless treatment he receives from his newly empowered older daughters but, as the story continues, readers begin to realise that      has inflicted terrible damage on Ginny and Rose in the past. Unlike Shakespeare's play, *A Thousand Acres* shows that the tragedy is that of the daughters rather than the father and it is a tragedy that Smiley unfolds with great skill.

📽**Film version:** *A Thousand Acres* (1997, starring Michelle Pfeiffer and Jason Robards)

📖**Read on**
*The All-True Travels and Adventures of Lydie Newton*; *The Greenlanders*; *Moo*
David Wroblewski, *The Story of Edgar Sawtelle*

# ART SPIEGELMAN (b. 1948)

## MAUS (1972–91)
Comic books have long embodied America's view of itself. The first Golden Age of American comics came during the late 1930s and 1940s, with the arrival of the do-anything superheroes who could protect the nation in times of war and danger. In the 1980s, under the shadow of nuclear threat and as a new breed of Americans reclaimed culture, a new generation of 'graphic novels' emerged. From the subversive *Watchmen* to Frank Miller's *The Dark Knight Returns* and Robert

Crumb's collaboration with ›› Charles Bukowski, these works convinced many mainstream critics that comics could be literature. But if one graphic novel sold them for good, it was Art Spiegelman's 1992 Pulitzer Prize-winning *MAUS*. Artist and illustrator Spiegelman was nurtured in the underground comics subculture of the 1960s and 1970s. He went on to forge an academic career and found the avant-garde *RAW* magazine, in which *MAUS* was serialised. The series, then book, portrayed his Jewish parents' survival in Hitler's Europe. Its masterstroke was that, in stark black-and-white imagery, Spiegelman drew the Jews as mice and the Nazis as cats. The result is a moving, thoughtful and unique piece of work that, as well as portraying inescapable fear, reflected upon the deep impression the Holocaust etched into the consciences of later generations and its survivors. What makes *MAUS* so extraordinary is not that it is a graphic novel, but that it finds a new approach to much written about events. Like Orwell's *Animal Farm*, *MAUS* seems to suggest that some things are so indescribably horrific, their imagery so indelible, that to understand them afresh we must find a new language – in both of these cases, animal allegory. So many authors expend thousands of words in painting a picture of American and Jewish experiences; Spiegelman did it with more immediacy and impact than most of them could ever hope to achieve. No wonder that, after 9/11, it was Spiegelman who designed the now famous *New Yorker* cover of a pair of black, silhouetted twin towers.

## ☙Read on

*In the Shadow of No Towers* (Spiegelman's response to the events of 9/11)
Will Eisner, *A Contract with God*; Joe Sacco, *Palestine*

# WALLACE STEGNER (1909–93)

## ANGLE OF REPOSE (1971)

Wallace Stegner has often been described as the greatest writer of the American West and it is certainly true that much of his life's work in fiction, history and biography has been devoted to chronicling the West but it would be wrong to consider him as little more than a regional writer. Perhaps one of the reasons Stegner's huge achievements as a novelist have not received the same attention as those of some of his contemporaries is that they have been too often hidden under the limiting label of 'Western writer'. Stegner began to publish his fiction in the 1930s and gained his first significant success in 1943 with *The Big Rock Candy Mountain*, the story of a violent drifter dragging his family from town to town in search of a fortune that always beckons but never arrives. He published more than a dozen other novels of which the best-known is *Angle of Repose*. This is the book of which Stegner himself once wrote, 'It's perfectly clear that if every writer is born to write one story, that's my story'. Winner of the Pulitzer Prize for Fiction in 1972, it is narrated by Lyman Ward, a retired and disabled history professor who is writing a book about his grandmother Susan Burling Ward, a writer and artist in the latter years of the nineteenth century who gave up the life she led in New York to follow her husband, an engineer, as he is despatched from job to job on the Western frontier. Lyman has taken on the task of writing his book to distract him from the deepening shadows in his own life and, as he meditates on the meaning of his grandparents' struggles, so his sense of his own place in the world changes. Through two intertwining narratives, Stegner creates a masterly book that reflects the deep connections between past and present.

**≋Read on**

*The Big Rock Candy Mountain; The Spectator Bird*
Peter Taylor, *A Summons to Memphis*

# JOHN STEINBECK (1902–68)

## THE GRAPES OF WRATH (1939)

John Steinbeck won the Nobel Prize for Literature in 1962 and his bibliography contains works which range from a re-telling of the Arthurian legends (the posthumously published *The Acts of King Arthur and his Noble Knights*) to an epic story of two families and their intertwining fates in early twentieth-century California (*East of Eden*) but his fiction is most closely associated with the 1930s and the Great Depression. His best-known book, *The Grapes of Wrath*, has become the classic fictional account of the suffering and social upheaval of the period. As the novel opens, its central character Tom Joad has just been released from prison on parole and he makes his way back to the family farm in Oklahoma, only to find that, after a ruinous crop failure, it has been repossessed by the banks who lent the Joads money. The family has no option now but to pile their few goods on to a truck and head out west. In doing so, they learn that they are like thousands of others who are making the same journey, seduced by the promise that jobs and the good life await them there. *The Grapes of Wrath* follows the family's trek to California and the gradual disillusionment that accompanies it. California is not the land of milk and honey they believed it to be. All the migrants, including the Joads, face exploitation by unscrupulous employers and, when they attempt to unite to combat that exploitation, they face violence and repression. Tom Joad is driven outside the law and forced to go on the run but, before he leaves, he promises his mother that the fight for justice will continue. Steinbeck's great novel reveals his belief in the power of ordinary people to cling to their humanity whatever the hardships they have to suffer.

**Film version:** *The Grapes of Wrath* (1940, directed by John Ford and starring Henry Fonda as Tom Joad)

**Read on**
*Cannery Row*; *East of Eden*; *Of Mice and Men*
T.C. Boyle, *The Tortilla Curtain*; Erskine Caldwell, *Tobacco Road*

# HARRIET BEECHER STOWE (1811–96)

## UNCLE TOM'S CABIN (1852)

When Abraham Lincoln met Harriet Beecher Stowe he is supposed to have remarked, 'So, you're the little woman who wrote the book that started this great war'. It's difficult today to appreciate fully the impact *Uncle Tom's Cabin* had on the American people and on public opinion worldwide in the decades after it was first published. It was, by some way, the bestselling American novel of the nineteenth century and, although it drew criticism from the very beginning, particularly for the passivity of the long-suffering Uncle Tom, its effect was remarkable. The author, Harriet Beecher Stowe, came from a family that played an important role in the religious life of nineteenth-century America and in the abolition movement. Her father and several of her brothers were preachers and authors who were known nationwide. *Uncle Tom's Cabin* was her first novel and, although she wrote others (*Dred: A Tale of the Great Dismal Swamp* is a second anti-slavery story), none was even remotely as successful. The characters – the martyred Uncle Tom himself, the villainous slave owner Simon Legree who so hates Tom's faith that he strives to beat it out of him, Eliza, the girl who makes her escape from slavery by leaping across the breaking ice of the Ohio River – took root in the American imagination on first publication and they are still there. The story, of slaves being sold down the river and separated from their families, of desperate attempts to escape and the cruel punishments inflicted by people like Legree on those recaptured, is familiar and unforgettable. *Uncle Tom's Cabin* and the innumerable adaptations of it that have proliferated over the years may have perpetuated harmful stereotypes about black people. However, its importance as a central text in the history of American literature, and indeed in the history of the American nation, is hard to deny.

## 📖Read on

*Dred: A Tale of the Great Dismal Swamp*
Harriet Jacobs, *Incidents in the Life of a Slave Girl* (glimpses of the reality behind Stowe's fiction in the memoir of an escaped slave)

# DONNA TARTT (b. 1963)

## THE SECRET HISTORY (1992)

To date Mississippian Donna Tartt has written only two books in two decades, *The Secret History*, published in 1992 when she was in her twenties, and *The Little Friend* which appeared ten years later. However, the huge success of her first novel alone announced Tartt as a new literary *wunderkind*. In *The Secret History*, poor Californian Richard Papen wins a scholarship to a prestigious Vermont college. He seeks out classics professor Julian Morrow, who takes a closed class of five handpicked intellectuals, including the chilly and enigmatic Henry and the effusive and arrogant Bunny. The latter, we discover in the opening, is destined to be murdered on an icy mountainside by the others. As Tartt gradually reveals why Bunny had to die, Richard falls deeper under the group's sinister spell. A brief précis may make Tartt's tale sound like a literary version of *Dead Poets Society* but its completely unsentimental storytelling and Greek mystery put it closer to John Fowles' *The Magus*. And it has plenty of echoes of earlier American literature: its creepy twins are reminders of ›› Henry James's *The Turn of the Screw*; the rationalisation of murder recalls ›› Highsmith's Ripley; its macabre high-tragedy is all ›› Poe. Richard is a blank-canvas narrator who seeks out more extreme individuals to enlighten his low-income, middlebrow life; his flaw is 'a morbid longing for the picturesque at all costs'. In the process he gives in to the bloody insanity of the group. The clash of Richard's classless West Coast background with the classical romanticism and snobbery of old East Coast America goes right to the heart of a schism that still exists. And there is that wealth divide: in one gripping section Richard nearly freezes to death alone, unable to support himself without his wealthy friends. The publishing experience of Tartt epitomises late twentieth-century American literature at its best (innovative and elegant writing, rooted in its heritage) and worst (overwhelming hype followed by writer's block). Yet Tartt's book is so perfectly conceived and engagingly told that it rises far above those commercial/literary hits that have graced television book clubs to become part of a much older canon.

**Read on**
*The Little Friend*
>> Jeffrey Eugenides, *The Virgin Suicides*; >> Patricia Highsmith, *The Talented Mr Ripley*

# JOHN KENNEDY TOOLE (1937–69)

## A CONFEDERACY OF DUNCES (1980)
*A Confederacy of Dunces*, a picaresque black comedy set largely in John Kennedy Toole's home town of New Orleans, was the only major work that this original but ill-fated writer produced. He wrote much of the novel in the early 1960s and then faced difficulties in getting it published. Many publishers expressed admiration for his manuscript but none the less turned it down. One major firm seemed set to add it

to their list but then withdrew. Despairing of ever seeing his novel in print and overwhelmed by other problems, Toole killed himself in 1969. It was only because of his mother's determination and her insistence that her late son had written a masterpiece that *A Confederacy of Dunces* eventually came to be published eleven years later. It went on to win the Pulitzer Prize for Fiction. The novel's chief protagonist is the gargantuan slob, Ignatius J. Reilly, a self-proclaimed genius in revolt against society in general and the city of New Orleans in particular. Ignatius is scornful of the notion of work and he lives in a fetid room in his mother's house, passing his time by masturbating, playing the lute and scribbling brilliant thoughts on a succession of supermarket notepads. Eventually his mother insists that he take a job but the consequences of Ignatius's greater engagement with life are disastrous. Bored after an hour in a factory, he sets about destabilising staff-management relations; hired to sell hot-dogs, he eats his stock; in all innocence, he takes up with drug addicts, whores and corrupt police. As his central character stumbles through a modern world with which he is ill-prepared to cope, Toole introduces readers to a vast cast of supporting players and weaves together a whole series of sub-plots into a rich and satisfying narrative. Toole's short, sad life may have ended in suicide but, in *A Confederacy of Dunces*, he produced one of the great American comic novels.

## ≋Read on

*The Neon Bible* (Toole's only other work, published after the success of *A Confederacy of Dunces*, was written when he was a teenager)
>> Michael Chabon, *Wonder Boys*; >> Walker Percy, *The Moviegoer*

# MARK TWAIN (1835–1910)

## THE ADVENTURES OF HUCKLEBERRY FINN (1884)

According to >> Ernest Hemingway, 'All modern American literature comes from one book by Mark Twain called *Huckleberry Finn*' and certainly Twain's novel, with its first-person narrative in the voice of Huck himself, opened up new ways of telling distinctively American stories. Hemingway may have exaggerated his case slightly but the influence of Twain's picaresque tale has been strongly felt for more than a century. Huckleberry Finn had already appeared as a major character in Twain's 1876 novel, *The Adventures of Tom Sawyer*, in which he was eventually rescued from life as the outcast son of the town drunk and adopted by a kind-hearted elderly lady. In the later novel, he tells the story of what happens to him after he has been taken in by the Widow Douglas. His boozy father reappears in his life and reclaims him. Weary of Pap's brutality, Huck fakes his own death (he kills a pig to provide the necessary blood) and escapes. He then joins forces with the runaway slave Jim and they take a raft down the Mississippi. As they journey down the river, they encounter a variety of rogues, vagabonds and fellow travellers. They meet up with two con-artists who pull them into their schemes to fleece the gullible and eventually sell Jim back into slavery. Huck and Tom Sawyer, who arrives unexpectedly on the scene, set about rescuing him. After a series of improbable coincidences and revelations, a happy ending seems to have been reached. But Huck, embodiment of the longing for freedom, remains unconvinced of the benefits of what the future holds. 'I reckon I got to light out for the territory ahead of the rest,' he confesses in the last lines of the book, 'because Aunt Sally she's going to adopt me and sivilize me, and I can't stand it.' Often very funny, *The Adventures of Huckleberry Finn*, with its unrestrained use of what would now be considered racially offensive language, can also make uncomfortable reading for a modern audience. It remains an inescapable presence in American literature – a novel that explores ideas of race and freedom and identity which still echo down the many years since it was written.

**Film versions:** *The Adventures of Huckleberry Finn* (1939, starring Mickey Rooney in the title role); *The Adventures of Huckleberry Finn* (1960); *The Adventures of Huck Finn* (1993, starring Elijah Wood in the title role)

**Read on**
*The Adventures of Tom Sawyer*; *A Connecticut Yankee in King Arthur's Court*; *Pudd'nhead Wilson*
Joel Chandler Harris, *Uncle Remus*; William Dean Howells, *The Rise of Silas Lapham*; ➤➤ J.D. Salinger, *The Catcher in the Rye*

# ANNE TYLER (b. 1941)

## THE ACCIDENTAL TOURIST (1985)

Anne Tyler has been publishing her fiction since the 1960s and her novels have been shortlisted or won most of the major literary prizes in the USA. *Breathing Lessons*, for example, the deceptively simple story of husband and wife Ira and Maggie Moran, unfolded on the single day in which they drive to the funeral of an old friend and back home, won the Pulitzer Prize in 1989. Her plots are often as straightforward as those of a romantic novelist but her books have a grace and an emotional depth that few romances can match. The danger for a writer in focusing on the everyday and giving it space is that she records instead only the banal, highlighting the kind of mundane material that fiction usually edits out. There is never any such danger with Anne Tyler. Her fiction may deal with the ordinary but it does so in extraordinary ways. Although it was *Breathing Lessons* that won the Pulitzer, *The Accidental Tourist* has some claims to being her best novel. The story centres on Macon Leary, a writer of a series of travel books for people who don't really like to travel but are forced to do so for their work. Like his readers, Macon doesn't much enjoy travelling. In fact, since the murder of his twelve-year-old son, he doesn't much enjoy anything. The grief he and his wife have experienced after their tragedy has driven them apart rather than brought them together and she has left him. He is living alone, desperately aware that he is becoming, as his wife informs him before her departure, 'a dried up kernel of a man that nothing real penetrates'. Tyler's novel follows Macon as he struggles to rebuild his life and to understand what he feels about Muriel, the unconventional woman he meets when he takes his dog to the Meow Bow Animal Hospital. Touchingly funny and perceptive, *The Accidental Tourist* shows Anne Tyler at her very best as a novelist.

📖**Film version:** *The Accidental Tourist* (1988)

📖**Read on**
*Back When We Were Grown Ups*; *Breathing Lessons*; *Dinner at the Homesick Restaurant*
Jane Hamilton, *The Book of Ruth*; Alice Hoffman, *Seventh Heaven*; Alison Lurie, *The War Between the Tates*; Anita Shreve, *The Weight of Water*

# JOHN UPDIKE (1932–2009)

## RABBIT, RUN (1960)
After a false start as a cartoonist, John Updike began his writing career producing short stories, primarily for *The New Yorker*, in the late 1950s. *Rabbit, Run* was only the second novel he published. Over the next half century, Updike published an astonishingly wide variety of other fiction. *Couples* follows a small group of bored Connecticut commuters who change sex-partners as carelessly as if playing a party game; *The Witches of Eastwick* sees three young widows set themselves up as a

coven of amateur witches, only to become sexually ensnared by a devilishly charming man; *Gertrude and Claudius* is an ambitious and witty retelling of events familiar from *Hamlet*. However, during these years, whatever other fictional paths he trod, Updike returned again and again to the everyman figure he created in *Rabbit, Run* – Harry 'Rabbit' Angstrom, a former school sports champion who finds emotional maturity and happiness almost impossible to grasp. In the first of the sequence, Harry is in his late twenties and, his glory days as a high-school jock already behind him, he is feeling trapped by marriage and career. Janice, his wife, no longer excites him and his job as a salesman in the fictional Pennsylvanian town of Brewer is dull. Harry makes an ineffectual attempt to escape the hand fate seems to have dealt him by getting in his car and driving out of town but all he does is get himself lost. He rapidly ends up back in Brewer where, estranged from Janice, he embarks half-heartedly on an affair. Nothing that life offers seems as fulfilling as his days as a basketball champion but, in his flailing attempts to find happiness, Harry does little except create further anguish for himself and others. Written in the present tense, *Rabbit, Run* thrusts readers into the midst of its central character's confusion and allows them to see the pains of this ordinary man with the compassion of an insider.

## 📖Read on

*Rabbit Redux* (the next instalment in the story of Harry Angstrom); *Couples*; *Roger's Version*; *The Witches of Eastwick*
>> John Cheever, *The Wapshot Chronicle*; >> Richard Yates, *Disturbing the Peace*

# GORE VIDAL (b. 1925)

## BURR (1973)

In the sixty years since his debut with *Williwaw*, a story of the war in the Pacific written when he was still in his teens, Gore Vidal has published more than twenty novels and has also produced screenplays, detective stories, political polemics and some of the best American essays of the last hundred years. He is known for fiction as different as *Julian*, an historical novel about the last pagan Roman emperor, and *Myra Breckinridge*, a gender-bending account of the excesses of the film industry. However, there is an argument to be made that his finest achievement as a storyteller is the long, interconnected sequence of novels about the rise to great power status of his native land which is usually known as the 'Narrative of Empire' series. The first of these is *Burr* which tells the story of Aaron Burr, third vice-president of the USA and one of the more colourful politicians from the early years of the new nation, a man whose career only foundered when he killed Alexander Hamilton, one of his greatest rivals, in a duel. Vidal has always prided himself on his iconoclasm and *Burr* provides an unsurprisingly idiosyncratic view of the Revolutionary era. His leading character is usually dismissed as (at best) an embarrassment or (at worst) an out-and-out villain in traditional accounts of American history but, in Vidal's story, he is the hero. Seen through the eyes of Charlie Schuyler, the journalist looking back on his career, and in the fictional memoir which Vidal creates for him, Aaron Burr is a larger-than-life figure brought down by lesser men. It is the hallowed founding fathers like George Washington and Thomas Jefferson who are portrayed as idols with feet of clay. *Burr* is an appropriate opening volume for the 'Narrative of Empire', the series of seven books in which Vidal punctures some of the most comforting myths about America's past.

### ⪨Read on

*Lincoln*; *1876* (the next two novels in chronological sequence in the 'Narrative of Empire'); *Julian*
Louis Bayard, *The Pale Blue Eye*; ≫ E.L. Doctorow, *Ragtime*; ≫ Jane Smiley, *The All-True Travels and Adventures of Lydie Newton*

# KURT VONNEGUT (1922–2007)

## SLAUGHTERHOUSE-FIVE (1969)

Twenty-two-year-old Kurt Vonnegut was in Dresden as a prisoner of war when the Allies rained fire upon the city in February 1945. This tragic, unnecessary destruction etched an indelible image on the mind of the young Indianapolis-born soldier and, twenty-three years later, it informed his extraordinary fourth novel, *Slaughterhouse-Five*. In the book, Billy Pilgrim, the gangly, unremarkable son of a barber from Ilium, New York, is 'unstuck in time'. His adventures, told without adherence to chronology or narrative conventions, include two key moments: his presence at the destruction of Dresden as a POW, locked in a meat locker, and his kidnapping by bizarre aliens from the planet

Trafalmadore, who perceive the universe in four dimensions and time as a mass of continually existing simultaneous moments. 'All time is all time,' they say, 'it does not change.' Around these two events Vonnegut weaves Billy's random, tragic, ridiculous life, ending with a murder based on a lie. 'So it goes', as the fatalistic refrain that rings throughout the novel has it. Vonnegut breaks rule after rule in his humorous, sad satire. Billy is a passive figure, while his time-jumping ensures that each event is a chance happening of laughable absurdity, rather than building suspense – this is a Trafalmadorian novel in which fate is the main character and Billy and Vonnegut just pawns. (As in the metafiction of >> Paul Auster, or >> Jonathan Safran Foer, the author inserts himself into the narrative.) For all its metaphysical fatalism over mass-massacre – as a result the novel remains controversial in America – this is an anti-war novel in which choice still counts: in its closing moments Vonnegut reminds us that the war was ending as Dresden was bombed, and shows us the shooting of poor Edgar Derby for merely stealing a teapot. Yet Vonnegut's most impressive achievement is to show fiction's inability to talk meaningfully about events as cruel and insane as war. Just as Monty Python's *Life of Brian* is film's most incisive examination of organised religion, *Slaughterhouse-Five* shows that to understand something as absurd as random murder, one must oneself become absurd.

So it goes.

🎞**Film version:** *Slaughterhouse-Five* (1972)

🔖**Read on**
*Breakfast of Champions*; *Galapagos*

>> Philip K. Dick, *Ubik*; >> Jonathan Safran Foer, *Everything is Illuminated*; >> Joseph Heller, *Catch-22*; George Saunders, *Civilwarland in Bad Decline*

# ALICE WALKER (b. 1944)

## THE COLOR PURPLE (1982)

Alice Walker was born in Georgia, the child of a poor farming family, and won college scholarships which provided opportunities to escape the poverty and limitations of her background. In the 1960s she became an activist in the civil rights movement and later worked as a journalist and editor. Her first book, a collection of poems, was published in 1968. Her debut novel, *The Third Life of Grange Copeland*, followed two years later. She has had a long and productive career as both poet and novelist but her greatest success, both critically and commercially, has been with *The Color Purple* which won the Pulitzer Prize for Fiction and went on to become a Spielberg-directed Hollywood movie. The book tells the story of Celie, a young black girl in the American Deep South in the 1930s. As a teenager, Celie is raped and abused by the man she believes to be her father. She gives birth to a child which her father sells. Then he marries Celie off to the brutal widower 'Mister' and her sufferings continue. He beats her and forces her into near slavery in the service of himself and his children from his previous marriage. Only when she meets the glamorous singer Shug Avery is Celie able to break out of the trap her life has become and find the love and fulfilment she has always been denied. Now she can re-establish contact with Nettie, the sister she loved and lost, whose parallel story of life on a mission in Africa is revealed. By the end of the book, Celie's journey from abuse and disempowerment to a position where she can celebrate the joys and riches of life is complete. Told through a series of diary entries and letters, and notable for its eloquent use of black American vernacular, *The Color Purple* is a remarkable and inspiring book.

**Film version:** *The Color Purple* (1985, directed by Steven Spielberg and starring Whoopi Goldberg)

**Read on**
*Possessing the Secret of Joy*; *The Third Life of Grange Copeland*
Ernest J. Gaines, *The Autobiography of Miss Jane Pittman*; **»** Toni Morrison, *The Bluest Eye*

# DAVID FOSTER WALLACE (1962–2008)

## INFINITE JEST (1996)

David Foster Wallace's suicide at the age of only forty six deprived contemporary American fiction of one of its most ambitious and innovative practitioners. His first novel, *The Broom of the System*, emerged from his graduate work at Amherst College and was published in 1987 to acclaim from several national critics. He went on to produce several volumes of shorter fiction but the only other major novel he published in his lifetime was the monumental *Infinite Jest*. Set at some point in the not-too-distant future (since the book was published in 1996, readers now may well be living in the years Wallace was anticipating), the book takes place in a North American state known as ONAN (the Organisation of North American Nations) which consists of the current USA, Canada and Mexico. The plot focuses on a movie of the same name as the novel which is so entertaining that, once people have seen it, they have no desire in life other than to keep watching it. The film is the work of James Orin Incandenza, a deranged and deceased genius who also founded the Enfield Tennis Academy, location for many of the novel's finer moments. Incandenza's hugely dysfunctional family, plus the members of a halfway house for addicts, find themselves drawn into a plot by the leader of a Quebecois separatist movement to use the film to destabilise the government of ONAN. Just as wild and demented as any plot summary can suggest, populated by a cast of thousands and provided with hundreds of offbeat footnotes to accompany its action, *Infinite Jest* is a uniquely original work of fiction. There may be an argument to be made that

Wallace was more gifted as a digressive and vastly erudite essayist than as a novelist. Certainly collections of essays such as *A Supposedly Fun Thing I'll Never Do Again* contain some of his finest writing. However, *Infinite Jest* deserves its place in any list of the best and most surprising works American literature has to offer.

🐟**Read on**
*A Supposedly Fun Thing I'll Never Do Again* (essays); *Brief Interviews with Hideous Men* (short stories)
William Gaddis, *The Recognitions*; ▶▶ Thomas Pynchon, *Vineland*; Neal Stephenson, *Snow Crash*

# NATHANAEL WEST (1903–40)

## THE DAY OF THE LOCUST (1939)

Born in New York of German Jewish parents from Lithuania, Nathanael West spent years managing small hotels and putting up writers, including ▶▶ Dashiell Hammett, and working as a cartoonist. The everyday lives he observed in hotels came to life in four short but subversive books in which the striving for 'life, liberty and the pursuit of happiness' becomes a destructive impulse. West's vicious Hollywood satire *The Day of the Locust* was published in 1939, when West was living in Tinseltown – he moved there to work on an adaptation of his novel *Miss Lonelyhearts* and stayed as a jobbing scriptwriter. Its central character is the artist turned set-painter Tod Hackett, who is struggling with work for the picture *The Burning of Los Angeles* when he meets Faye Greener, a coquettish blonde wannabe. Around this manipulative young woman circles a coterie of eager men, including a truculent dwarf, a cowboy, a Mexican and a former hotel bookkeeper named Homer Simpson. Homer is a doltish man, starry-eyed with longing for Faye, and he lets her move into his home, with disastrous consequences. The Hollywood of *The Day of the Locust* is wholly false, a set of brittle illusions beneath which lie envy and sexual aggression. Everyone wants to be a star or possess one and no one is genuine – even Tod fantasises about raping Faye – except Homer Simpson, the victim and the key figure in the story. Homer is the guy at the bottom, the man who came to California, like the people in the crowd rioting at a movie premiere at the end of the novel, full of hope and, fed a constant diet of lies by the media and movies, found only misery. 'They were savage and bitter,' West writes, 'and had been made so by boredom and disappointment.' Like Evelyn Waugh and ›› F. Scott Fitzgerald, West wields his pen with a sharp disdain for the social forces that rip the humanity out of people. Tragically, in December 1940 America lost two of its greatest authors, when Fitzgerald and West, only thirty seven, died on the same weekend. Yet in this funny, savage novella, West left us with what may well be the truest Hollywood tale ever written, a warning about the corrosive cult of celebrity that we have continued to ignore.

**Film version:** *The Day of the Locust* (1975, directed by John Schlesinger and starring Donald Sutherland)

**⮑Read on**

*Miss Lonelyhearts*

>> F. Scott Fitzgerald, *The Last Tycoon*; Horace McCoy, *They Shoot Horses, Don't They?*; Budd Schulberg, *What Makes Sammy Run?*

## READ ON A THEME: HOORAY FOR HOLLYWOOD?

John Gregory Dunne, *Playland*
Henry Farrell, *Whatever Happened to Baby Jane?*
>> F. Scott Fitzgerald, *The Last Tycoon*
James Frey, *Bright Shiny Morning*
Elmore Leonard, *Get Shorty*
>> Norman Mailer, *The Deer Park*
Theodore Roszak, *Flicker*
>> Jane Smiley, *Ten Days in the Hills*
Terry Southern, *Blue Movie*
Michael Tolkin, *The Player*

# EDITH WHARTON (1862–1937)

## THE AGE OF INNOCENCE (1920)

Upper-class New Yorker Edith Wharton was a literary star by the time *The Age of Innocence* was published in 1920 thanks to her satirical tragedy of 1905, *The House of Mirth*; among those the gregarious writer and style-maker regularly entertained was her great friend ▶▶ Henry James. A well-travelled woman, she was devoted to France, remaining there after an unhappy marriage, working with refugees during the war and writing her Pulitzer Prize-winning *The Age of Innocence* there afterwards. Newland Archer, the book's hero, is a young lawyer from a prestigious New York family, and is engaged to pretty, perfect May Welland. When May's disgraced cousin the Countess Olenska arrives, she gets Manhattan 'society' chattering, yet charms Archer with her enlightened European ways and modern forthrightness. Their clandestine love highlights the aggressive shallowness of New York's rarified elite of the 1870s. This is a society on the brink of extinction: immigrants and youth are ushering in a new *laissez-faire* European culture, while the 'old' families are dying out. Wharton preserves an earlier time in aspic in order to dissect it with scalpel-like penmanship, satirising the protectionism of anachronistic Victorian manners. Yet buried within the clutter of cultural artefacts she portrays with biting humour is a tragic love affair that is genuinely moving. In this respect, the title applies ironically to the surface generosity of those that treat Countess Olenska so vilely and stand between her and Newland. But there is a second meaning: this was the last hoorah of a generation that would vanish with the First World War and whose focus on the minutiae of social convention – so richly portrayed in the novel

– was not merely ridiculous to enlightened souls like Wharton, but positively grotesque in the context of the young men rotting in the killing fields of Europe: only in 'innocence' could such complacency exist. Wharton's genius was to combine deep characterisation with intense period detail to remind us, finally, that however shallow these shadows of Wharton's childhood, the loss of their innocence was the great sadness of the twentieth century.

**Film version:** *The Age of Innocence* (1993, directed by Martin Scorsese and starring Daniel Day-Lewis and Michelle Pfeiffer)

**Read on**
*The House of Mirth*
William Dean Howells, *A Modern Instance*; >> Henry James, *The Wings of the Dove*

# THORNTON WILDER (1897–1975)

## THE BRIDGE OF SAN LUIS REY (1927)

In his lifetime, Thornton Wilder was as famous as a playwright as he was as a novelist. *The Matchmaker* (the play on which the musical *Hello, Dolly* was based), *Our Town* and *The Skin of Our Teeth* were all Broadway successes and the last two won Pulitzer Prizes for Drama. He wrote seven novels of which two are still well worth reading. *The Ides of March* is an historical novel which, charts in a series of imaginary letters, the converging destinies of a group of people in Ancient Rome: it ends on the morning of the Ides of March 44 BC, as Julius Caesar sets off for the senate house and the assassination that, we know, awaits him there. Wilder's best-known novel, which appeared twenty years before *The Ides of March*, was also historical fiction but it was set in eighteenth-century Peru. The focus of the book is the collapse of a bridge which propels five people to their deaths. Wilder, supposedly drawing on the research of a Franciscan monk who witnessed the accident, charts the lives of each of them and the small, seemingly random moments of fate which lead them to the instant at which the bridge gives way. They are a disparate group of people – from a Marquesa and her companion to the son of an actress – but they are united in death. The monk who saw them all fall is haunted by what he has seen and what it seems to say about destiny and divine intervention in human affairs. He spends years attempting to prove that there was more to the collapse of the bridge than mere chance but he fails in his self-imposed task to explain the deaths. In the final analysis, we can only accept that, as someone says at the end of the novel, 'There is a land of the living and a land of the dead and the bridge is love, the only survival, the only meaning'.

## ☙Read on

*The Ides of March*
>> Willa Cather, *Death Comes for the Archbishop*

# TOM WOLFE (b. 1931)

## THE BONFIRE OF THE VANITIES (1987)

Tom Wolfe made his name as a leading proponent of New Journalism in the 1960s. The most famous of his literary non-fiction books is *The Electric Kool-Aid Acid Test*, published in 1968, which exposes truths about the 'peace and love' represented by Ken Kesey. Wolfe's first novel *The Bonfire of the Vanities* appeared in 1987 after serialisation in *Rolling Stone* magazine and announced a fiction author unafraid to tackle controversial socio-political subjects. Having dissected first the hippie era and then the 'Me decade', Wolfe became *the* chronicler of the 1980s. It begins as wealthy Wall Street investment banker and self-proclaimed 'Master of the Universe' Sherman McCoy is involved in a hit and run in the Bronx. Driving his Mercedes is his mistress; the victim, a young black man, is fatally injured. As the case explodes, Sherman is descended upon by vultures who want to use it to their own ends, including an alcoholic journalist, a self-aggrandising prosecutor and a power-crazed Harlem pastor, all of whom pick at the bones of the banker's disintegrating life. Wolfe's New York is the world's centre, 'the Rome, the Paris, the London of the twentieth century, the city of ambition, the dense magnetic rock, the irresistible destination of all those who insist on being *where things are happening*'. In an infamous clarion call in *Harper's* magazine after the book's publication, Wolfe argued for the vitality of the realist novel in the style of Zola, Thakeray and Sinclair Lewis. It is indeed an extraordinary argument for the novel as reportage: he shows how minorities are held back by local greed and political manoeuvring, how the justice system is swayed by individuals, and how the media hungers for flesh. Twenty years on, Wolfe's didactic narrative may be literally too black and white, but it makes its points with great verve, wit and a remarkable eye for detail. From the roar of the trading floor to that of the Bronx expressway, Wolfe's masculine, propulsive novel is a full-formed picture of 1980s New York, both a supreme entertainment and a sophisticated argument for fiction as social chronicle and conscience.

**Film version:** *The Bonfire of the Vanities* (1990, starring Tom Hanks as Sherman McCoy)

**Read on**
*A Man in Full*
>> John Dos Passos, *Manhattan Transfer*; Adam Haslett, *Union Atlantic*; >> Jay McInerney, *Bright Lights, Big City*; Richard Price, *Clockers*

# RICHARD WRIGHT (1908–60)

## NATIVE SON (1940)

Richard Wright started life inauspiciously. Born on a Mississippi plantation in 1908, abandoned by his sharecropper father at five and with a paralysed mother, convention would have written off the uneducated, poor African-American. Instead, he took a post-office job in Memphis and taught himself from books in the 'whites only' library, before moving to Chicago in 1927. There he became a writer and a Communist Party member and married a white woman. Then his 1940 novel *Native Son* brought him literary fame. *Native Son* bursts with controversial power – Wright is not interested in telling a sentimental story of triumph over adversity· he wants the truth. Bigger Thomas is a petty-stick-up man in 1930s Chicago's South Side ghetto. There he lives with his mother and siblings in a rat-infested tumbledown one-bedroom 'garbage dump' owned by white liberal millionaire Mr Dalton, with whom he gets a job as a chauffeur. Powerless to change his family's suffering, Bigger's shame, guilt and fury mean that: 'He knew the moment he allowed what his life meant to enter fully into his consciousness, he would either kill himself or someone else'. Bigger bubbles with potential criminal energy: for how can one not act guilty when one is born guilty? When the crime comes, it's an accident of the worst kind: the murder of Mary Dalton, the rebellious, drunken daughter of his employers. And so the entire system turns on Bigger. This gripping book is a masterpiece of social observation provocatively centred on an essentially unsympathetic character – and Bigger is a fully rounded character, not a cipher – whose actions are guided by hate, fear and lust. Wright confronts labyrinthine issues that are as depressingly relevant now as then: the hypocrisy of the liberal white elite; white authorities' indifference to the spread of black-on-black crime; the role of young male African-American culture in fostering both crime and violence towards women; systemic dehumanisation of the African-American criminal. *Native Son* is a towering achievement and a touchstone for African-American literature that can still be read as a damning indictment of power and race relations in America today.

🎞**Film versions:** *Native Son* (1951, starring Richard Wright himself as Bigger Thomas); *Native Son* (1986)

📖**Read on**
*Black Boy* (Wright's autobiographical account of growing up black in Mississippi); *The Outsider*
>> James Baldwin, *Go Tell It On the Mountain*; Chester Himes, *If He Hollers Let Him Go*

# RICHARD YATES (1926–92)

## REVOLUTIONARY ROAD (1961)

In the past decade, Richard Yates made one of the great posthumous literary comebacks. A native New Yorker, his stories won prizes throughout the 1950s, and his first novel, *Revolutionary Road*, was nominated for the National Book Award in 1962. But then Yates vanished from the public consciousness, until a new edition and Sam Mendes' film adaptation reminded the world of his mastery. Summer, 1955. Frank and April Wheeler have it all: the beautiful young family, the perfect Connecticut home, the well-paid job. Beneath the surface, however, complacency, distrust and bitterness are eating away at their marriage. Children came too soon; both have abandoned the dreams they sold each other upon; Frank is having an affair. When April comes up with a plan for them to move to Paris to escape suburban suffocation, Frank's limitations doom their marriage. Yates is flawless in realistically portraying the passive-aggressive disintegration of a marriage built on incorrect assumptions and the slow, unspoken breaking of promises. The Wheelers have, in keeping with their middle-class milieu, found myriad distractions to make living a lie bearable, from building a new garden path to having children. His psychological insight into the self-deceiving Frank, in particular, is acute and moving, his imagined conversations with April at odds with the spiky reality. The Wheelers' actions are sadly diminished versions of their abandoned ambitions and reflect parental issues: April, once a promising young leading lady, is reduced to appearing in a disastrous amateur dramatic production – a reflection of her deep need to re-embody the glamour of the irresponsible parents who left her. Frank, meanwhile, yearns to prove himself intellectually but feels compelled to live up to his father's masculine ideals; he's cut out for neither. Both are sympathetic in isolation, tragic and cruel together. *Revolutionary Road* continues the subtle, character-driven dissection of class and gender seen in ›› Wharton and ›› Fitzgerald, in which the individual identity is subdued via a series of intricately woven inventions – and like them, his insight into the personal price paid in pursuit of the American Dream must earn him a place in the literary canon.

**Film version:** *Revolutionary Road* (2008, directed by Sam Mendes and starring Leonardo DiCaprio and Kate Winslet)

## Read on
*The Easter Parade*
›› John Cheever, *The Wapshot Chronicle*; Rick Moody, *The Ice Storm*;
›› John Updike, *Couples*

# INDEX

# Other books in the 100 Must-Read Series

Discover your next great read ...

*100 Must-Read American Novels*
Nick Rennison, Ed Wood
9781408129128

*100 Must-Read Books for Men*
Stephen E Andrews,
Duncan Bowis
9780713688733

*100 Must-Read Classic Novels*
Nick Rennison
9780713675832

*100 Must-Read Crime Novels*
Nick Rennison,
Richard Shephard
9780713675849

*100 Must-Read Fantasy Novels*
Stephen E Andrews, Nick Rennison
9781408114872

*100 Must-Read Historical Novels*
Nick Rennison
9781408113967

*100 Must-Read Life-Changing Books*
Nick Rennison
9780713688726

*100 Must-Read Prize-Winning Novels*
Nick Rennison
9781408129111

*100 Must-Read Science Fiction Novels*
Nick Rennison, Stephen E Andrews
9780713675856